BUBBA on BUSINESS

Common sense from working people about respect, accountability, and results

Dennis W. Melton & David C. Dunn

Copyright 1998;2020 by Dennis W. Melton and David C. Dunn

All rights reserved. No part of this publication may be reproduced, distributed, or transmitted in any form by any means, including photocopying, recording, digital, online, or other electronic or mechanical methods, without the prior written permission by the publisher, except in the case of brief quotations embodied in critical reviews and certain other noncommercial uses permitted by copyright law. For Permission requests, write to the publisher, addressed "Attention: Permissions Coordinator," to the address below:

1134 Battery Lane
Nashville TN 37220
615-289-9505

Bubba on Business: Common Sense from working people about Respect, Accountability, and Results / Dennis W. Melton and David C. Dunn

ISBN 9798835424870

PREFACE

This book is about achieving business results in partnership with people – People like Bubba.

Bubba is everyone

The central factor in this story, as in any real organization is 'Bubba.' Some may view the name Bubba as derogatory; a term, like "redneck" or "hick" intended to poke fun at working people, especially Southerners. Nothing could be farther from our intent. We *like* Bubba, we respect him, and we know that Bubba is the one who really makes any business successful.

"Bubba" describes a perspective, not a stereotype. Bubba is a fictional stand in for the great majority of people – those who work hard, care enough to get frustrated, and do their best in most situations. In this book Bubba is a technician in a manufacturing plant, but Bubba can be found in every office, hospital, shop and retail store.

Workers' wisdom through storytelling

Rather than write a typical business book, we've woven a fictional story, based on real incidents, that illustrates the process of making the workplace better. We've marked a few of the more unbelievable actual situations and comments with an asterisk (*). Naturally we changed names, places and enough detail to protect anyone from embarrassment. Most importantly, the results described are real. They can be – and have been – achieved by any organization that is willing to act on the principles outlined in Bubba's story.

Change your organizational culture

The process we describe involves shaping workplace culture – the system that governs how people get things done at work. The system includes the personalities, behaviors and skills of people; the policies and practices; the decision-making process; the communication channels; and the informal way "things are around here."

We believe that Bubba and the vast majority of working people are keen observers of how the workplace really operates. Bubba's wisdom comes from real-world experience. Unfortunately, most managers don't take time to listen to Bubba, and thus miss a vital source of ideas and opinions – not to mention support for business results. This wisdom, what we call "Bubba on Business," is key to improved business results.

Dennis W. Melton

David C. Dunn

THANKS

To God, without Whose divine intervention our partnership and this book would never have been.

To our wives, Julia Dunn and Ginger Melton, without whom our work and travel would be overwhelming: Thank you for making our homes a haven. To our kids, Rebekah and David Dunn Jr. and Katherine and Matthew Melton: Thanks for thinking we are special – at least most of the time.

To our parents, Sonny and Jo Dunn and Wade and Delline Melton. Your love, sacrifices, work ethic, and common-sense teaching laid a foundation for our lives and for this book.

To Mike McDermott and Ed Rachie, original partners in Ninety-Five/Five, who laid the foundation of the 95/5 Philosophy.

A special thanks to Sheldon Bowles (co-aurthor of Raving Fans and Gung Ho!) for his interest in Bubba, and to Rick and Carolyn Crandall of Select Press. We appreciate the time energy and enthusiastic support they devoted to making *Bubba on Business* better.

Finally, we extend our sincerest thanks and appreciation to our clients, too numerous to mention individually. It is their openness, passion for making things better, commitment to the 95/5 principles, and willingness to listen to their own "Bubbas" that has created positive workplaces for their employees.

CONTENTS

Preface
Thanks
Seeing the Impact   1
Bubba Speaks Up   8
Pursuing Change   18
A Curve in the Road   27
Redesigning the System   43
Great Expectations   54
Taking it Personally   64
Winners & Losers   71
Ensuring Accountability   83
Making a Difference   92
Getting Results   109
Final Thoughts   117
Appendix A   120
Appendix B   124
Appendix C   127
Who wrote this book?   130

SEEING THE IMPACT

The workplace is a system. But who is it designed for; and what results does it produce?

****

"Most people want to do what's right. But they get fed up." – Bubba

---

1

Wham! The break room door nearly came unhinged, and Bubba Self jumped three inches out of his seat as the press crew entered. It sounded like a riot. Mingled snatches of conversation with hard-core profanity reached Bubba, but he could only catch phrases. One thing for certain: these boys were *mad*!

"Two hours overtime *every day*! And Saturday on top of *that*! They can't do that! I always thought Sonny was one of us, and now he's. . . ! *I can't work over . . . I got class tonight.* Well, I guess you'll just get fired . . . or maybe just suspended. That's what they do when you try your best around here. *He's got some nerve tellin' us we got to work over, when he just suspended our best operator!*"

This ain't fair

"Hey! What's up?" Bubba called out over the din.

Chair legs screeched on the tile as Jerry and Henry pulled up to Bubba's table. "I'll tell you what's the up," Jerry practically shouted. "*You heard about Sam gettin' suspended this morning for makin' a mistake? Well, now they tell us we've all got to work overtime to make up for it. Every day for the next two weeks, *and* this coming Saturday!"

"But one man can't make *that* much difference," Bubba said.

"That's right," said Henry, "but when we've got people like Jimmy, Harold and Barb that ain't here but half the time, orders are way behind. Sam could do more than five of them, and he was keepin' our head above water. And look what he got for his trouble!"

"Well at least he got three days away from this place!" a young hand said with a smirk.

"You don't understand, Ricky – all you're workin' for is a truck payment while you're livin' at home with mama. Sam's *got* to work, cause he's got a family. That three days' pay hurts him," Jerry scolded. Others nodded. "Sam ain't never been a minute's trouble to anybody. This ain't fair."

"To him *or* to us," said somebody else in the crowd.

"It looks like the ones that don't want to work don't have to, and the ones that tries just has to do more and more," said Henry. "And if you do make a mistake, it don't matter how good a worker you are or how hard you try. You get the same as if you didn't try at all."

"That's right," agreed Jerry. "Makes you want to quit trying."

"*Or just quit, period,*" Bubba thought.

2

Marty Peoples, Plant Manager, shifted restlessly in his chair as he finished his notes for Sam's file. He always hated the paper trail requirement of their disciplinary process, but usually they were deserved. Sometimes people straightened out; sometimes they didn't. But in his 14 years as a manager with Specialty Products, he'd never had one bother him like this one.

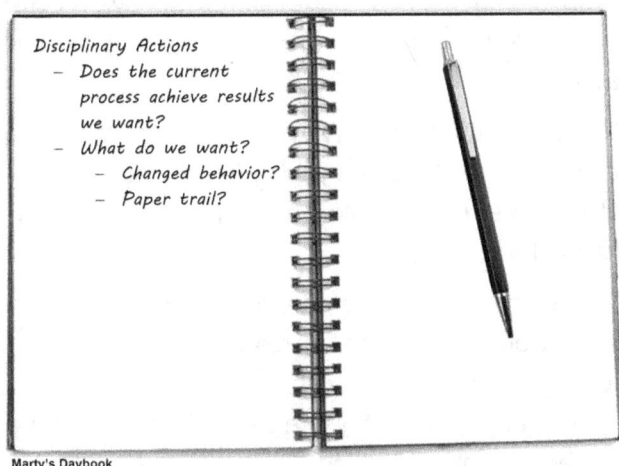

Marty's Daybook

"Sam's a good employee," Marty thought. "He's always here, and always on time. He works hard. He doesn't complain... but he broke the rules. It wasn't his fault, and it wasn't my fault. I had to enforce the rule - otherwise we'd have chaos..."

His thoughts were interrupted by Sonny, the press room supervisor. "I'm headed out Marty," he said. "See you're finishing Sam's write-up. I hated to do that. He's the best operator I got, and we're already behind.

"Yeah, Marty replied, I hate it for him, but it's one of those things that as plant manager
... well, you have to do sometimes." He stopped just short of saying, "*One of those stupid things you have to do.*"

The workplace system: People, policies, and practices

"Some of the folks are pretty upset about what we did." Sonny said. They didn't think he deserved a suspension for a safety violation – and they sure don't like mandatory overtime. I rekon you have to enforce the policy, or there isn't any point in having one, right? It's Management 101 – you have to treat everyone exactly the same, regardless of history or circumstances, no exceptions.

"Yeah, that's the way you have to look at it," he replied half-heartedly. Marty finally looked directly at him. "How often have you had to write up somebody when you didn't think it was fair?"

"More than I want to," Sonny said. "But this was for Sam's own good, too. I mean, double-loading a die on the press is dangerous. He could have been hurt, and he could have damaged the tool. Maybe he didn't do it on purpose, but if somebody breaks a rule, they have to be punished. We can't play favorites. I'll bet Sam will remember this for a long time."

"Yeah," Marty said. "That's what I'm afraid of. Will he remember how important safety is, or how we treated him - an employee with a spotless record?"

"If we made an exception for Sam, some jerk would claim we have to make one for him, too," Sonny said. Marty's mind drifted as he doodled in his pocket daybook: ***Do rules for the jerks mean the jerks rule?!***

"But why do we let the jerk drive our decisions for us?" Marty asked. "A jerk who's been *this* close to being fired every year for 10 years, but just keeps slipping through loopholes?"

"Yeah, but Marty, we write the jerks up, too. It's just

that it doesn't do any good. They don't *mind* being written up. All we can do is follow the rules," Sonny replied. "We don't make 'em. Look, if we don't follow the rules the jerks will be running the place."

And that, Marty decided, was *precisely* what was happening here. He jotted his thoughts in his daybook:

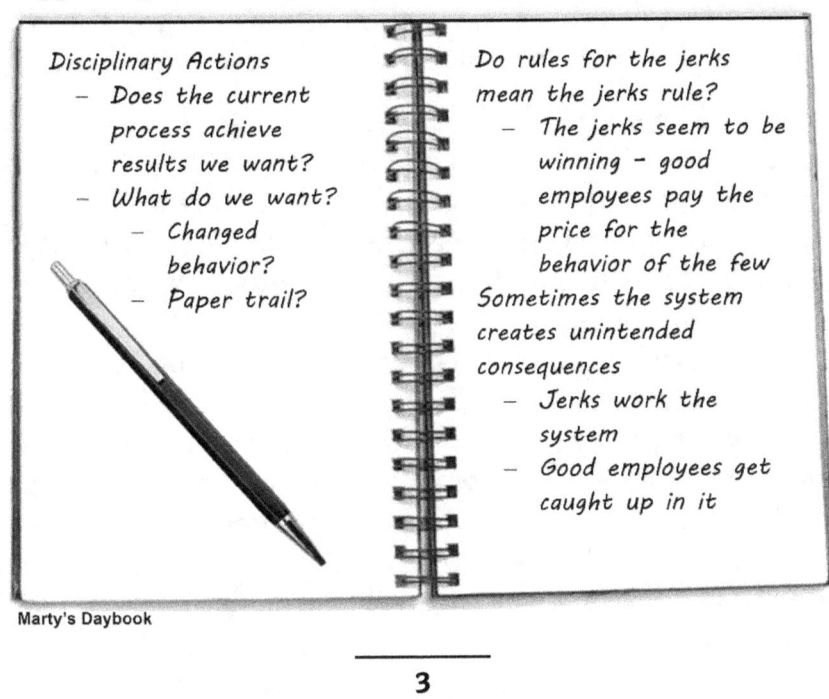

Marty's Daybook

3

The next afternoon, Henry and Earl were talking quietly at their workstations as Bubba approached.

"What's going on?" Bubba asked . . . Earl snickered, choked back a laugh, then erupted.

"Earl saw Jimmy at lunch," Henry responded, tight-lipped with disapproval.

"But Jimmy's out today – again," Bubba said.

"I know," said Henry, obviously unamused. "He showed up at the smoking area after lunch. Tell him, Earl."

"You better keep this to yourself, you hear!" Earl whispered. "He just said to be watching at the time clock about 10 minutes till quitting time."

Sure enough, at the appointed hour Jimmy showed up at the time clock outside Sonny's office.

"Jimmy, where in blazes have you been?" demanded Sonny. You didn't call in again. You knew if you had one more point on your attendance, we'd have to fire you." Jimmy slowly reached for his timecard in the rack, inserted it in the clock, and handed it to Sonny with a sly smile.

"Sorry I'm *late*, boss," Jimmy drawled. It took a moment for Sonny to realize that, by clocking in late – even seven hours, 50 minutes late – Jimmy would only receive *half* a point under the attendance system and would keep his job. And one point would come off tomorrow – it's been 30 days since his last warning*. He'd played the system and won again. Sonny's face began pulsating like a faulty neon sign.

"Just get your . . . over there and get to *work*!" Sonny stammered, struggling to control his language if not his emotions. "At least you'll be working two hours over tonight with everybody else!"

> Beating the system is a game for some: "I win, you lose."

"I can't work over tonight. I have bowling league. Besides," Jimmy said pleasantly, "the policy says we have to get four hours' notice or it ain't mandatory. I hate to let you down, but I didn't get four hours' notice." With that, Jimmy ambled to his work area giving a wave to Marty who was watching from his office. Marty, who had been watching from the office, stared for a moment and turned away. Sonny and the crew returned to business, a couple laughing and most shaking their heads.

Watching this, Bubba wondered if he should go ahead and talk to Marty. He didn't want to make Marty angry. *"But,"* he thought, *"if this don't show there's a problem, what will?"*

BUBBA SPEAKS UP

Arbitrary rules designed to stop a few malicious people more often actually "catch" good employees.

****

"I hope you don't think I'm out of line, but I don't think it's fair to start with." – Bubba

4

Marty looked up to see Bubba standing silently just outside the door. He seemed nervous, his fingers gripping the brim of the cap he held in his hand. No knock: no greeting – just standing there.

"What can I do for you, Bubba?" Marty said tiredly. He glanced at the clock and saw that Bubba's shift had just ended. "Oh, I don't need set-up to stay over, just operators and packers. You can go on home."

"No, sir, that ain't what this is about," Bubba said. "I don't mean to stick my nose in where it ain't welcome, but I came to talk to you about Sam."

"Oh," Marty said. "Come on in and sit down." As Bubba entered, Marty added, "Now, you know I can't talk about a personnel situation involving another employee. That wouldn't be fair to him."

"Well, I hope you don't think I'm out of line, but I don't think it's fair to start with," Bubba said. "Now, I know *you* can't really discuss it, but *I* need to say some things just for me. And the thing that's got me upset is that this was Sam's first problem since he come to work here. Marty, how long you been knowing me?"

Marty sat back. Bubba had been one of the first operators he met when he transferred to the plant nearly 10 years ago. Bubba was smart and committed and everybody seemed to listen to him. Marty had recommended Bubba train as a technician, and he'd made a good one. "Ever since I got here, Bubba," he said.

Advice worth listening to

"I like workin' for you Marty," said Bubba. But I have to tell you that I think you did wrong suspending Sam. He made an honest mistake, and he's losing three days' pay for it. Meantime, there's folks like Jimmy that have been laying out of work for years, and they're still workin'."

As Bubba mentioned Jimmy, a cold chill ran down Marty's back. And it wasn't just the incident moments before. Jimmy had been disciplined, suspended, and chewed out countless times. But it didn't seem to do any good. He seemed to enjoy confronting Marty and the supervisors – it seemed his mission in life was to stay in management's face. Like today, just when Sonny had a fleeting hope that they *had* him, Jimmy would find some loophole to get out of it. Or he'd do better just long enough to have the violation removed from his file, and then do it all over again. It was as if *policies were written for Jimmy's personal benefit!*

"The way I see it, there's just a few around here that's causing the real problems," Bubba continued, "but it's the majority like Sam that has to pay for them."

Marty opened his daybook and penned a note.

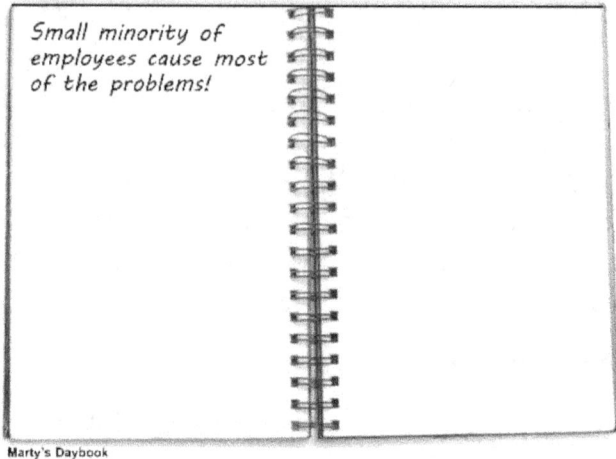

Marty's Daybook

"Bubba, you know I can't talk specifically about Sam or about Jimmy, but what percent of our folks would you say really seem to be causing problems over and over?"

Bubba looked surprised. "Marty, you know 'em as well as I do. Chuck and Barb are the worst ones to miss work. And Jimmy... well, you know all about him. Harold and Missy are here most days, but they're late two or three times a week, and they always seem to have a problem with production or quality. They keep me back there all the time, saying their machine ain't right. I'd say it's less than 10 percent of the people – maybe about 5 percent." Marty added to his note:

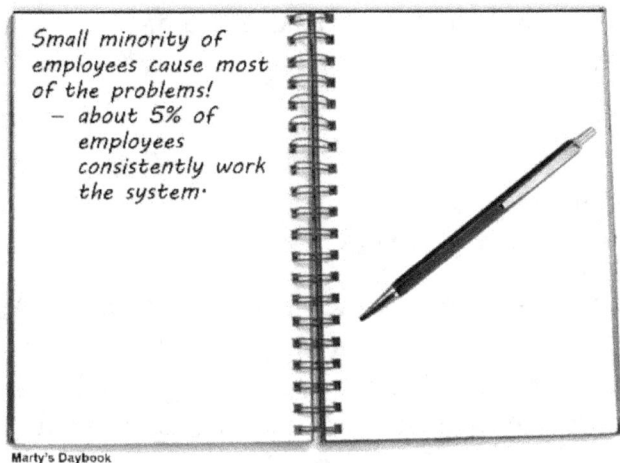

Marty's Daybook

Bubba chuckled. "I remember ol' Fred Harrison used to have a problem, too."

"Yeah, but we let him go," Marty interjected.

"After 15 *years*!" replied Bubba. "And the only reason you got him then was 'cause he lost count of how many days he could miss before his last warning dropped off."

Milking the system

Marty was stunned. "You mean, people actually *calculate* how many days they have to wait before missing again?"

"Why sure," said Bubba, a bit shocked at Marty's question. "Barb's even got a calendar at her machine with the next day she can miss circled in red ink! You never seen that?" Marty had to admit he'd never looked.

"Barb and Missy not only know their attendance; they know everybody *else's* attendance. They even take turns missing sometimes. They're pure geniuses at finding ways around the rules. If they spent as much energy doing what they were supposed to as they do figuring ways to get out of work, they'd own this place by now."

People notice

"If it's only about 5%, why are other people having trouble, too?" Marty asked.

"Because people notice what happens, who gets by and who gets nailed," Bubba said. "People say, 'Well, if they can lay out or goof off, I will, too'. Most people want to do what's right, but they get fed up." Bubba lowered his voice. "Like what happened to Sam. Marty, I think you ought to call Sam in and warn him, then bring him back. He won't do it no more. The rest of us would appreciate it."

"Will they?" Marty asked. "If I let Sam get by, everybody will want to get by one time. Everybody'd shout, 'Favoritism!'

"Wait a minute," said Bubba. "Everybody?" Who do you think would be the first ones wantin' to get by with something?" It's those same ones we talked about, the 5%. And besides, who do you think that rule was put in for, anyway?"

Marty thought a minute. "Well, it was to protect everybody. It's safety."

Bubba shook his head. "No. Matter of fact, I *know* who it was put in for. Ol' girl named Martha used to work here. She was the most careless person I ever seen. She'd double-load the press about twice a week. I think it was just to tear something up so's she could stand around. It didn't bother her one bit if she cracked a die or broke a bolt. So finally, they put in this rule to stop her from doing it."

"Did it work?" asked Marty.

"Yeah; stopped her from that trick, but she kept finding new ways to screw stuff up. She'd put stuff in backward, or she'd have such bad quality it would take us half a day to sort through her parts. She'd say that production was too high, or the material was bad – you know, any excuse."

"So, we put in a rule for somebody who was screwing up over and over, and then applied it to somebody else who made one mistake," Marty thought aloud as he wrote:

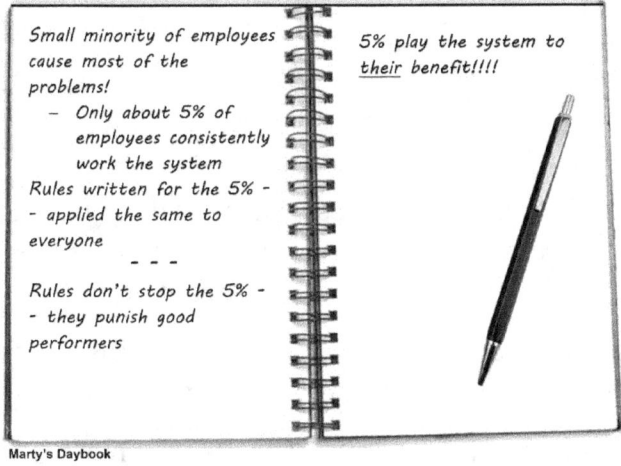

Small minority of employees cause most of the problems!
  - Only about 5% of employees consistently work the system
Rules written for the 5% -
- applied the same to everyone
- - -
Rules don't stop the 5% -
- they punish good performers

5% play the system to their benefit!!!!

Marty's Daybook

Marty looked up. "Bubba, you've given me something to think about. I don't know what I can do about Sam at this point, because I can't just change a rule. I'll talk to Human Resources, then I'll call Sam. But I want to think some more about this issue of who the rules were written for, and who they get applied to. I know that doesn't seem right, but we have to treat everybody equal."

"Why should we?" Bubba asked as he stood to leave. "Seems to me we ought to treat people according to how they *act*. When you give better, you ought to get better."

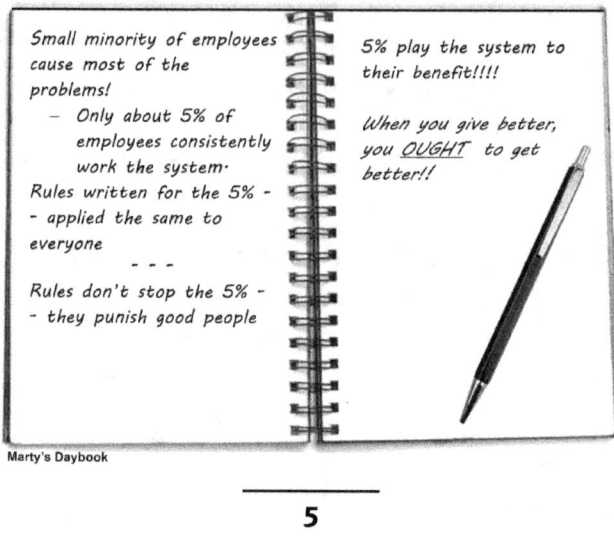

Marty's Daybook

5

"Pull up a stool, Bubba," bartender Roy called across the Palace barroom. "Mighty quiet this afternoon. The usual suspects ain't showed theirselves yet."

"Most of 'em are pulling some overtime at the plant," Bubba replied. "You ain't seen Sam Blount today, have you?"

"He was in here earlier. Mighty down in the mouth," said Roy. "Said he ain't felt so humiliated since he was a kid. It does seem a little bit harsh to me. Don't it?"

"Yeah, I think so," said Bubba. He looked at the corner table where Jimmy and some friends were playing cards and drinking, adding quietly, "Especially when folks like *that* can get by with most anything."

"Uh-huh," Roy agreed. "Hey, Jimmy, you been in here about all day. Don't you have to work?" he called out.

Jimmy laughed as he ambled over to the bar where

Bubba sat. "Well, I *did* work, didn't I, Bubba? For about five minutes," he said. "I just wanted to jerk ol' Sonny's chain a little. Keeps him straight. Besides, I don't like to kiss up to nobody. You know what I mean, Bubba?"

"No," Bubba replied simply. Jimmy's hand rested uncomfortably on Bubba's shoulder, but he resisted the impulse to slap it off. About that time, Bubba's brother Junior walked in. Jimmy moved his hand and nodded in greeting.

"I'll bet you were in there talking to your buddy Marty about me, or maybe poor ol' Sam," Jimmy said with mock sympathy. "You know, it's pitiful how they treated old Sam. I been telling you for years that sooner or later management will get you. See my idea is that if you screw up enough, they'll quit messing with you."

"Well, you set a high standard for the rest of us to follow," Bubba said. Roy choked back a guffaw, but Jimmy didn't laugh. Bubba turned toward Jimmy. "Tell me, how can you afford to be out of work so much when you ain't getting paid?"

> Most rules define the level of misbehavior you will tolerate, rather than setting a high standard.

"I just ain't for sale to no company that don't respect me," Jimmy said stiffly. "If they'd pay more, I'd consider being there more."

Bubba ignored the stupidity of this logic and pressed, "If you feel that way, why don't you quit?"

"Cause I'm having too much fun driving people like you crazy!" Jimmy laughed, slapping Bubba's back and walking away. "They can't fire me. What would you have to talk about? See you around, Mr. Company Man!" he mocked.

The 5% are everywhere

Junior sat down beside Bubba. "Junior, you all got any like him over where you work?" Bubba asked.

"They're everywhere, ain't they?" Junior replied as he poured his beer into a glass.

"But y'all have a union. Ain't that supposed to make it better for the workers?"

"Not when it comes to people like Jimmy. My job as steward is to make sure the company follows the contract and don't take advantage of the workers, but between you and I, it seems like I spend more time trying to get screw ups like him off the hook than helping people who deserve it," Junior said. "Most of the people and most of the supervisors are no trouble. But there's a few – workers and supervisors, too – just like him that make everybody miserable."

"Yeah, I was talking about that with Marty. He was asking about how many of our folks really cause trouble, and I figured it was about 5%, more or less," said Bubba.

Junior thought a minute. "Yeah, that's about right. Now, you've got a few ol' boys that will see what they can get away with once in awhile. But there ain't many of the ring-leaders."

So, what do you do about them?" Bubba asked. "They ruin the place for everybody else because most of the rules are made for them."

"When you figure it out, let me know," said Junior, draining his glass, "and we'll sell it! Bring me another one, Roy."

95/5 Principle

- **The vast majority of employees are good people.**
- **A small minority – about 5% - try to manipulate the system.**
- **Most systems are designed for the 5% who manipulate them, not the 95% who do their best.**

PURSUING CHANGE

The vast majority can see the symptoms created by a flawed system.
It is up to leaders to listen and then plot a different course.

****

"Folks ain't opposed to change when they see what's in it for them." – Bubba

6

A little after nine the next morning, Bubba figured Marty had really lost it.

There was Marty with his little book, writing as he walked. He'd stop and look – at a machine, a stack of boxes, posted notices on the bulletin board, the time clock – then he'd jot a note and mutter to himself. A couple of the guys got a kick out of Marty's actions. Everyone seemed in a better mood since Sam had been called back. Even Missy seemed glad about the decision. Of course, she may have been happy just to be standing around. Bubba had been listening to her all morning; her machine wasn't working right - again.

"Wonder what's with him?" Bubba said to Sam motioning toward Marty.

"I don't know, but he's been this way ever since before I got here," Sam said. "I told him I was glad to be back at work, and I appreciated another chance. By the way, some of the guys told me you went to bat for me, and I really appreciate it."

"No, I talked to Marty, but he had to handle it from there," Bubba said sheepishly. Just then Marty walked by, so Bubba figured he'd see what was going on.

"Marty," Bubba shouted, trying to catch up to him.

"Yes, Bubba?" Marty replied, looking up from his daybook.

"I really appreciate what you did for Sam," Bubba said, "but after what you said last night, I wondered how you were going to explain it to the 5%."

"I talked with Marilyn in Human Resources last night. I decided that you were right: the vast majority of people would appreciate us taking into consideration Sam's record, and I really didn't care right then *what* the 5% thought," Marty said. "After we looked at it, we realized that the length of the suspension was *up to* 3 days. I told her we needed to reconsider the policy, but in the meantime, this was one of those 'discretion of management' things. I'll take the heat, 'cause it was the right thing to do."

"So what in thunder you doing roaming the building like a cat burglar – or a peepin' Tom?" Bubba asked. "Are you checking up on us? We were wondering whether to call a lawyer or the nut farm."

"No, I haven't gone crazy, but I'm finding some things that might be making us *all* that way," Marty laughed. "If you have a minute to come in the office, I'll tell you."

"Well, maybe Missy can run without me for just a *few* minutes," Bubba said sarcastically.

7

"Let me tell you what I've been asking myself," Marty said. "Is high performance rational?"

"Huh?"

"Does it make sense to do your best, as opposed to the bare minimum?" Marty asked. "See, I was up last night thinking. Why is it that the majority seem to get jerked around by the rules put in place for the 5%? So, I came in and started looking for some things we do that actually reward the 5% and punish the good performers."

"What in thunder are you talking about?" Bubba asked.

Consequences influence behavior

"Consequences influence behavior," Marty explained. "We all naturally do those things that make life easier and avoid those things that make life harder. Problem is, many of Specialty Product's rules and policies seem to be geared to the 5%, so I wanted to see what kind of consequences people get around here."

"What'd you find? Bubba asked.

"Look here at my book," Marty said, handing his daybook to Bubba.

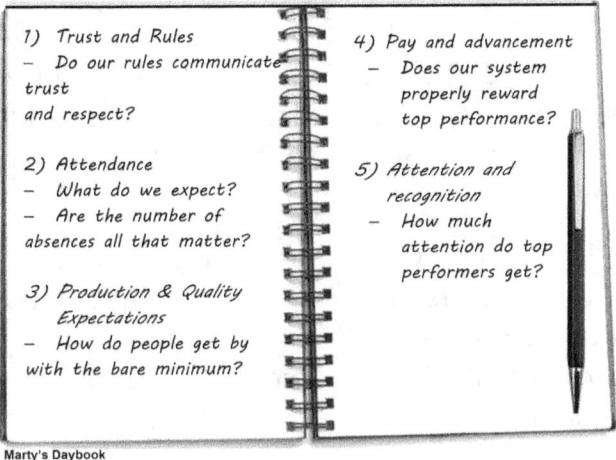

Marty's Daybook

"First, look at all the ways that we tell people, 'We can't trust you.' Why do we have time clocks? Because there are some people who would lie about their time. Does the clock keep people from missing work or being late?" Marty said.

> Trust and rules. What do our rules communicate?

"No, but it's harder to cheat," Bubba said. "Besides, every place has time clocks. Nobody minds that."

"I'll bet they mind doctor's notes," Marty shot back, and Bubba nodded. "How many times have people paid out money for a doctor visit just to get a note, just because our policy says you have to have a note or you'll get a point. The issue is, we treat everybody like they're in grade school."

"But we have to have rules, or Jimmy and his crowd would plumb shut us down," Bubba objected.

"Have the rules really changed their behavior?" Marty asked. "I've been here 10 years, and Jimmy's been the same regardless of how we change the rules. In the meantime, a lot of other good people who don't intend to break the rules get caught. Like Sam did on the press."

"*Or like Cathy," Bubba added. "Hadn't missed a day in 4 years, and then gets wrote up when her kid got in trouble with the law and she had to go to court with him a few times."

"That's what I mean," said Marty. "The rules we have aren't really working. They tell the 95% that we don't trust them, and the 5% just find a way around them. I can think of a dozen examples," Marty said, "but Cathy's case reminds me of my second point there:"

"What do we really expect about attendance?" Marty asked.

Attendance

"I guess we expect folks to be here," Bubba said.

"I thought that, too, but what does our policy say? If you think about it, it says there's a certain amount of time that's OK to miss."

"Well, of course, we have excused absences for sickness. . ."

"With a doctors' note," reminded Marty, "and those can be faked."

"And there's bereavement . . ." continued Bubba.

"Again, with proof of death – and we tell you how much your loved one is worth by specifying how much time you get," Marty interrupted again.

"So?" Bubba asked wondering where Marty was headed.

"The point is, we say we expect people here, but there's 30 reasons that we'll say it's OK if you aren't," Marty answered. "And if that isn't enough, we have a point system that says you aren't *really* in trouble until you cross a certain line. That line usually catches only the people who aren't watching, because they don't intend to cross it."

"And folks like Jimmy who want to play games can find a way around it," Bubba added.

"So, again, is it more rewarding to come to work every day, or to try to find that line and get as much time off as you can?" Marty asked. "Now, think about the this:"

"Who has it easier – high performers or marginal performers, those who only want to do the minimum?"

Bubba thought about his experience with Missy. Other operators would handle variations in material and changes in design by themselves, but every little deviation drove Missy crying to Bubba. *'Bubba, I just can't make this stuff come out right! This piece of junk they gave me won't do right. I can't be responsible for making production if they won't get a new machine'* . . . or *'get the right material'* or *'quit changing the way they want it done'* or something.

> Is high performance rational?

What did Missy get for her antics? Well, a lot of Bubba's time, for one. And she got to stand by the machine while he worked on it. If the press supervisor asked her to sweep or make boxes while Bubba worked, she griped. Then she'd sweep for a minute, and off she'd go to the bathroom or the break room.

Meanwhile, when Sonny the press supervisor needed something done in a hurry, who got the job? Yep – good old reliable Sam, or Henry if Sam was busy, sometimes Marge or Cathy. Sometimes if all of them were behind, Sonny would do it himself rather than ask Missy to do it. After all, he'd just have to do it over again anyway.

"From a work standpoint, the better performers have it harder," Bubba replied. "They get to do harder work, and more of it. And when things don't go right, who do you get upset with? The good performers."

"I hate to admit it, but I've done it myself when the pressure's on," Marty said. "And who gets left alone to do what they please?"

"The 5%," Bubba said, remembering Jimmy's remarks at the Palace: '... *if you screw up enough, they'll quit messing with you.*'

"But good employees get higher increase at their review, and they get the promotions," Bubba objected.

"That's true to a point," Marty said. "But let's look at pay and rewards."

"The 5% make close to the same money. And money can't be what's important to them, or they'd be at work more. And as for promotions . . . when was the last promotion here?"

| Pay & Rewards |

Bubba thought. "I guess when Sonny got to be press supervisor," he said, "and probably mine before that."

"And that's been two years," Marty added, "so promotions aren't that frequent? So, to my last point, who gets the lion's share of. . . ?"

> **Attention & Recognition**

". . . time and attention?" Bubba filled in. The 5%, right? I see what you mean Marty. But you're a good guy. The other managers are OK. It ain't your fault. The 5% just stir up trouble. That is just the way it is. My brother Junior says it's the same at his place, too."

"I appreciate your saying that it's not my fault, but it *is* the system's fault. And I'm part of the system that puts consequences on the backs of people who are doing their best, while the 5% gets away with it. We have to change the system to put the consequences in the right place," Marty said firmly.

> **Pursuing Change**
> - **Consequences influence behavior**
> - **Do the consequences for high performers make sense?**
> - **People notice who gets by and who gets nailed.**

TO DO LIST

- ☐ Make time to talk with top performers. Tell them you appreciate what they do.
  - BE SPECIFIC!
  - Ask them what they get for their efforts
  - Build a relationship – Let them know you trust and respect them.
- ☐
- ☐
- ☐
- ☐

A CURVE IN THE ROAD

Change, for people and companies is a process that begins with seeing the problem and understanding the consequences.

****

"Change is tough to start, and tough to keep up." – Bubba

8

Bubba crashed through the swinging doors of the Smyrna Hospital Emergency Room and stopped, sweeping the room with his eyes to find someone he could question.

"Over here, Hon!" His eyes followed the sound, spotting his wife Dottie who worked as an aide at the hospital.

Bubba walked briskly around the desk over to a curtained cubicle. Under the curtain he could see the feet of a man and a couple of women. Their movements seemed paced and their voices casual, so he hoped this was a good sign.

"How is he?" Bubba asked in a loud whisper.

"He'll be all right. Fractured forearm, separated shoulder, bruised ribs," she said as she embraced Bubba. Looking him squarely in the eye, she added, "He was real lucky. *Real* lucky this time."

The doctor extended his hand, "Hello, Bubba. Dottie was working here in the ER when they brought him in," he said. "He's looking better."

"Can I talk to him now?" Bubba asked.

"I suppose," said the doctor. "He's alert but may be in some pain until the medicine takes effect."

"Bubba." Dottie gripped his sleeve and said quietly, "His blood alcohol was .15! The deputy said drinking caused the wreck. He hit the ditch and flipped; barely missed a tree."

Bubba nodded silently. *"It's not the first time,"* he thought as he squeezed her hand and slipped through the curtain.

Junior sat shirtless on the table in a semi-upright position, talking with a female attendant. His left shoulder, arm and side were raw and blue, with a clean white cast on his forearm suspended from a sling. Not bad, considering.

"Hey, Junior," Bubba interrupted. "Glad to see you're well enough to flirt."

"I guess it just wasn't my time to go, huh?"

"Not *this* time, I reckon," said Bubba sternly, "but what about next time?" Lowering his voice, he added, "Junior, how much had you been drinkin'?"

"You ain't gonna start on me about *that* again, are you?" Junior whined. "I stopped by after work at the Palace, just like you do."

"Yeah, and I know Roy wouldn't let anybody get in such a shape they couldn't drive. Do you know what your blood alcohol level was? You had a .15! Are you telling me you only had a beer at the Palace?"

"Well, I stopped at the store and got a 12-pack and some cigarettes," Junior said. "I might have had one or two more. Look, all I drink is beer. I ain't no alcoholic. A few beers ain't never hurt nobody."

"Well, they nearly *killed* you!" Bubba said.

"I ain't hurtin' nobody but myself," Junior shot back. "Nobody cares nothin' about this ol' country boy."

"Tell that to the folks at the plant that wanted you to be steward," said Bubba, "and to Carol and the kids. They only left 'cause o' your screamin' and cussin' after you'd been drinking."

"I never hurt *nobody!*" Junior screamed.

"Not with your hands! They were just scared you were going to tear the place up and leave them with nothin'! Or show up at work drunk and lose your job. Or maybe just kill your fool self, like you almost did tonight" Bubba said in a muffled, trying-not-to-scream-in-public whisper.

Junior just glared.

"And I'm scared of losing you, too." Bubba softened his tone. "Junior, why can't you see what this is doing to you? What's it going to take to make you change?"

"It ain't nobody's business but mine," said Junior. "I can do what I want, when I want, and I can stop drinking when I want. Maybe I made a mistake. I had an accident, all right? I don't need to change nothing. 'Cept my underwear." Junior laughed, then grimaced at the pain.

For once, Bubba didn't laugh at a wisecrack so typical of the good nature that made Junior popular. *"Why can't he see?"* Bubba thought. *"Why's it so hard to change?"*

> Change is a process, not an event – for individuals <u>and</u> organizations

---

9

Work went smoothly the next morning. Bubba had finished the changeover on number 4 without a hitch. He'd even had time to unbox and shelve the replacement parts he'd ordered. "Yep," he thought as he got his tools out for the die change on number 8, "maybe a little too smooth."

"What's different?" he brooded. *"It seems like I've had time to do everything right on schedule – like there's something missing."*

"That's it," he said aloud. "Missy! She ain't called me in two days!"

"You talking to yourself, Bubba?" said Wayne.

"Oh, I reckon he misses his girlfriend," teased Sam.

"I wonder what's up with her. Is she out? Maybe she quit," Bubba thought, a bit hopefully before his conscience smacked him. *"Naw – I'd have heard that by now."*

A changed Missy

There she was. No sign of scrap parts. Finished parts falling into the bin in a steady, regular rhythm – the beat of a properly running, productive operator. Between cycles, she picked up finished parts, efficiently examined them under the light, and placed them in stacks.

This was Missy? *Our* Missy?

The break buzzer sounded, and she secured her machine, then noticed Bubba standing a little open-mouthed on the perimeter. "Hey, Bubba. She walked over. "Wanna go on break?"

"Uh, I reckon," he said. "You ain't called me today, or yesterday. Are you sure them parts are good?"

"Yep," she said proudly. "I've made production the past two days, and a good bit more. Everything's fine."

> **AWARENESS**
> Seeing the need is the first step toward change.

"But, that's not a usual thing," he persisted. "Usually, you uh ... have a lot of ... trouble."

"You mean, I'm usually a pain, right?" she said with surprising candor. Her voice dropped, almost apologetic. "I know. I have been."

They walked into the break room, and as they were sitting down, Bubba asked, "It ain't none of my business, but what made things different the past two days?"

"I got to thinking," she said, looking around at no one in particular. "My mama got laid off over at Tex-Made. You heard they were closing?"

"Yeah. Sorry. I didn't know your mama worked there."

"Well, I watched her over the weekend, how upset she was. She was saying how there was so many of the workers that, well, just didn't give a damn. Laying out, or causin' machines to break down so they could stand around. She said if more of them had done their jobs, maybe they wouldn't have closed," Missy said. "And I know she's worried about how she'll pay the insurance now. There ain't many hiring except the burger places and she can't do heavy work anymore.

"And looking at her, Bubba, I realized that I was one of *them* – the one's she was talking about that wouldn't half work. I saw what a good job meant to her; how much it hurt her to lose it. I know I need to help her now, and my brother. And, you know, this place ain't great, but Sonny and Marty ain't *too* hard to work for, the people are nice, and the benefits ain't too bad. So, I decided I was gonna do what I could to keep this place going."

> **UNDERSTANDING**
> Why it's important; the consequences of changing and of staying the same.

Bubba was stunned. "So, it took you seeing what happened to her to realize *you* needed to change? But – no offense – you knew you should have changed before, didn't you?"

"I guess I knew what I was doin' wasn't right, but I didn't really *understand why* I should change before. I didn't see what was in it for me. Maybe that's selfish, but I really couldn't see it. You know, that old song's right, 'You don't know what you got 'till it's gone'. Well, maybe I got smart in time to do something." She paused. "How's Junior? I heard about the wreck."

"I reckon he'll live awhile longer," Bubba tried to joke lamely. Even he didn't find it funny.

Missy's concern was genuine. "You remember me

and him dated for awhile until he started drinking a lot. Mama didn't think I should keep going with him. He's a nice guy. When's he going to stop drinking so much?"

"Well, I guess he hasn't seen what's in it for him yet, like you said," he replied.

"I'm worried about him, Bubba. Should I call? I don't want him to think, you know, the wrong way, but he's got to change, or he won't make it," she said.

"I wish Junior would start worrying about himself," Bubba thought. "Go ahead. See if you can get through to him."

10

"These numbers *have* to be wrong, Sonny," Marty insisted. "We've never been that close to production on 2108s. Are you sure they're actually in the warehouse?"

Sonny nodded. "Three skids of 'em, right where they're supposed to be. If we keep those slots full, I'll have to move the supplies I've been storing there."

"Yeah, if we get on target, it'll screw up your whole system, won't it?" Sonny laughed. "Hey, Bubba, you makin' those 2108s at home and bringing 'em in?"

Bubba took Sonny's call as an invitation to the impromptu production meeting. "Naw. That's the part runnin' on Missy's machine. She's caught up, and movin' ahead."

Marty was skeptical. "Sonny, have you inspected those parts? I don't want any returns because she's not paying attention."

Before Sonny could reassure him, Bubba broke in. "Marty, just relax. Your inventory's right, and the parts are on spec. Missy's just changed her way of looking at work."

"Yeah, that's all she's ever done – *look* at it," quipped Sonny, his eyes narrowing. "You been helpin' her?"

"No," said Bubba, "and I can see why you don't believe it. But look at the results: she's above production every day this week; she's at her machine on time, including after breaks and lunch; her work area's clean as momma's kitchen. She ain't called me all week, and she's running the new stock without a problem – or a complaint."

"It's got to be a miracle. Did she join a cult or something?" Sonny asked. "Now, don't make fun of her," Marty said. "Bubba, what *did* happen?"

"You might say she made a commitment. She said she appreciates her job more since her momma's been laid off at Tex-Made, and she decided to do what she could to keep it," Bubba

> **COMMITMENT**
> The third step in the change process comes from within. Ask people to commit to better performance.

said. "One thing's for certain: it ain't nothing we did. It had to come from her."

"Yeah, a commitment has to come from inside," questioned Marty, "but why change now? We haven't threatened her job."

"Didn't have to. She finally understood what was in it for her," Bubba said. "It hadn't ever been important until she saw her mama's situation. She saw where her path might be headin', I guess, and that kinda shook her up. Hey, y'all ought to stop by and tell her how good she's doin'. It's awful hard to change when you been doing it for years."

"Are you kiddin'? She might start screwing up again if we say anything," said Sonny.

"And that's why more people around here don't want to change," Bubba thought.

11

"Well, here come Slick and Slack now," Sonny quipped to Marty as Jimmy and Chuck rounded the corner from the break room – 10 minutes late.

"Late again," said Marty.

"Jimmy!" Sonny called, "could you come here a minute?" Marty was a little surprised that Sonny would say anything to Jimmy. He decided that he'd just stand back and watch the discussion unfold.

"Your time's my time, boss-man. What's the problem?" Jimmy said, knowing that anything Sonny might want to talk with him about *was* a problem.

"There's so many where do I start?" Sonny thought. "Uh, aren't you a little late getting back from break?"

"No. About the same time I usually get back," Jimmy replied.

"Oh. Well, everybody else was back 10 minutes ago."

"But Chuck and me were a few minutes late starting, cause we finished packing the order for the shipment at noon, like you said."

"Oh. So, how long were you on break?"

"About 10 minutes, like the handbook says."

"Well, if you were a couple of minutes late getting started, and only took a 10-minute break, how could you be 10 minutes *late* getting *back*?" Sonny's voice was perceptibly higher as his throat tightened.

"Oh, we took our 10 minutes in the break room, but then we went to the bathroom and we picked up some supplies on the way back," said Jimmy. "10 minutes is what we're supposed to get, ain't it?"

"Yeah, but . . . well, you should have been back on time. You need to make more of a commitment to your job, like everybody else," Sonny said.

"But we only were on break for 10 minutes, boss. How could we be late?" Jimmy smiled, sensing Sonny's imminent meltdown. "Listen, I got to get back to work. Chuck's way behind, and we can't miss that truck."

"Go on. But just be back on time from now on," Sonny lamely offered with a twist of artificial management authority at the end.

Think before you speak

Sonny knew he hadn't accomplished anything with Jimmy. Jimmy wasn't committed. He was obviously aware that he was late, and it didn't bother him.

Sonny turned to Marty, "Why can't I get through to him?"

"Well, one, he doesn't see the need to change," Marty replied. "And two, did you really know what you wanted to accomplish when you called him over?"

"What do you mean?" said Sonny.

"You wanted him to improve; to be committed. But had you planned what you wanted to say to Jimmy, and what you wanted to do about it?"

> **ACTION PLAN**
> A commitment without a plan is just good intentions: You need specific goals and a timeline.

"I guess I really didn't, "Sonny said. I just saw the situation and wanted to deal with it."

"How long did you think about what you wanted to say before you started?" Marty asked.

Sonny laughed. "Oh, about as long as it took him to get from the corner over here."

The game

"Exactly how many times has Jimmy been late?" asked Marty.

More than I can count. But I've done tried everything I know how to do," Sonny said defensively.

"I'm not blaming you," Marty said. I know it's frustrating, but my point is, he's been planning what he is going to say longer than you have. You just got run over."

"Is that what this is: a game of 'chicken'?" Sonny asked.

"To Jimmy, maybe it is. He's operating on the letter of the law," Marty said.

"So, 'what's in it for Jimmy?' means 'How can I beat Sonny by using his own rules against him?'"

"To a point, that's right. He's not asking what he *should* do. He's asking 'What's the *least* I have to do?' That's what all our rules tell him: the least he can get by with. He's just playing the rules against us," Marty said.

"And since he hasn't seen any reason to change anything, talking to him or telling him off isn't really doing any good is it?" Sonny observed.

Marty shook his head. "He doesn't understand what's in it for him yet. What's worse, everybody can see what he's doing. They see him scraping by, and it discourages them."

They realized this would take more than a casual conversation, or even a good chewing out – it would take a plan. Missy seemed to change when she finally realized the importance to her. Maybe Jimmy never would, but if there were any hope, it would come through understanding, too. He had to see that there were consequences of *not* changing.

12

Later that day, Bubba walked past Missy's machine. Her movements weren't quite as crisp as before. A small scrap pile had started, with parts on the floor. She put a part directly from the machine onto the finished stack without even glancing at it.

"Hey, girl," Bubba said. "Everything going OK?"

"Yeah, fine, Bubba," she said.

"You sure?" he said, trying to brighten the gloom. "You know, I was really impressed with you the other morning. Not many folks are willing to admit they've been wrong and do something about it. I was right proud to see the work you put into doing better."

Missy smiled. "You're nice to say that. you've been awful good to put up with me before." "I just wish somebody else would notice."

Change takes reinforcement

"Have you seen Sonny lately?" Bubba probed, hoping he'd stopped by after Bubba's suggestion that he compliment Missy on her new work habits. "I was lookin' for him."

"Yeah. I saw him awhile ago when he was counting my finished goods. I said, 'Pretty good production for me, ain't it?' and he looked at me and said, 'It's about time you was doing what we pay you for.'" She paused a moment and looked at him. "I know I wasn't much good before, but can't I get a little credit for tryin'?"

Bubba excused himself with a wave and strode off. He had something to say to Sonny.

Just behind the packing area, he got the opportunity. Sonny and Marty were sorting through boxes Chuck and Jimmy had packed wrong. The Lose Brothers were leaning against the wall absent-mindedly, watching the managers with their heads in the boxes comparing parts to packing lists. Bubba ignored Jimmy and Chuck's greeting and thrust his head into the large box.

"Sonny, I'm ashamed of you!" Bubba thundered at point-blank range inside the box. Sonny and Marty's heads bobbed up like birds on a lake.

"Don't do that, Bubba! Scare a fella half to death!" Marty gasped.

"What are you so ticked about?"

> "When people change in the direction you want, reinforce them."
> - Ken Blanchard
> *The One Minute Manager*

Sonny barked.

Jimmy and Chuck perked up. This was about to get interesting. Marty noticed the audience and said to them, "Hey, you guys have some re-packs to do, don't you?" They slunk over to the pile of parts. Marty then walked a short distance away, signaling with eye contact for Bubba and Sonny to follow.

"Sonny, I know you ain't convinced that Missy has really changed, but she was real disappointed when you told her, 'It's about time you started doin' what we pay you for'. Nobody in management's even noticed she's trying," Bubba said quietly.

"I ain't got time to hold her hand, Bubba, and you don't either," Sonny said defiantly. "If she gets consistent, I might say something to her at her review. But people don't deserve a medal for just doing their job a few days in a row. Think about Sam and Henry that's been workin' all along."

"But if we don't encourage her now, she won't ever be consistent. She's already starting her old habits; she's not bad yet, but not as good as she was when I first talked to her."

"See; I told you it wouldn't last," Sonny addressed Marty.

"Maybe not. But Bubba's right; she didn't deserve to be talked to like that. If we don't support her effort, she won't stick with it," Marty said. "And I should have said something, too. How long would you keep improving if people talked like that to you?"

SUPPORT
Resources and encouragement reinforce change

Sonny didn't answer.

"I'll go over this afternoon," Marty said to Sonny, "and you need to find the right opportunity to at least tell her you've noticed."

"If you both go over there falling all over her she'll know I said something," Bubba objected.

"Then we just need to be honest, tell her we should have said something earlier, but we didn't, and that we appreciate the good work," Marty said. "The truth usually works."

"Yeah, but make sure you notice *exactly* what she did," said Bubba. "Don't just throw out some half-baked compliment. Really look at her area, her parts, the way she organizes the material, her being on time – pick *something* that's really better. Something she's bound to be proud of."

"But won't it make her embarrassed or make her feel worse about the way she was?" Sonny asked.

"Not if you mean it," Marty said firmly. "And if you don't, don't bother. Now, go give our friends over there a clue net," he nodded toward Jimmy and Chuck, "and come by to see me when you're done."

Sonny walked back to lend Jimmy and Chuck an undeserved hand.

Other support

"Change is tough," Bubba said. "Tough to start, and tough to keep up."

"Yeah. I think we make it hard to give your best. I'm wondering what other support we need to give people,"

Marty mused.

"Whatcha mean?"

"Well, like our policies. Do they really support people who try their best, or just give folks like Jimmy some more chips for their game? And the way our managers deal with people. Sonny's a good guy, but he's frustrated having to deal with the 5%. I wonder what support I need to give him to get results, you know?" Marty was onto something. The next step would be interesting. "I need to finish the setup on 13. See ya," Bubba waved.

PURSUING CHANGE
- Change is a process, not and event – both for the individual and the organization.

- Five stages must be completed to create lasting change:
    - Awareness
    - Understanding
    - Commitment
    - Plan of Action
    - Support

- When change is introduced, everyone asks for the "WIIFM" (What's in it for me?)

- You create the WIIFM through making the aware of the need to change (the what) and helping them understand (the why and how) there is a need to change

- Commitment without a plan is just good intentions. Set specific goals and timelines.

- Establish support. As people change, it is often accompanied by frustration. Leadership needs to always provide support to help people succeed.

REDESIGNING THE SYSTEM

Traditional systems rely on rules that specify the worst we'll tolerate.
Effective workplaces set expectations and develop accountability by involving the 95%

****

"Lot's of folks want to make things better.
They're just waitin' for bosses
to listen." – Bubba

13

". . . so, you see, I'm convinced that part of our problem is that our policies and rules really tell folks how much *mis*behavior we'll tolerate. And we end up so frustrated that we really don't deal with problems. We just fuss and cuss, and hope they'll get better or quit."

Marty paused and looked at Marilyn, Specialty Product's Human Resources field representative from Headquarters. Mostly, she dealt with benefit problems, an occasional retirement, and a good deal of recruiting to fill vacancies. Once in awhile they called her about a termination or a workers' comp issue. Pretty routine stuff, normally. *This* – well, this was about strategy, about philosophy, about *change*.

Start with expectations

Marilyn was keeping her own counsel as she took notes studiously. *After all,* she thought, *this is a pretty good plant. Marty's proactive with people. Production is improving...*

Attendance had always been a problem . . . and always would be. They had some turnover, but with the kind of people you hire today, that's understandable. They're no worse than Specialty Product's other plants. That's what puzzled her about Marty's new drive. Why now?

"So," Marilyn finally lobbed to Marty, "what do you suggest we do?"

"I was hoping you might have some ideas," Marty replied. "I figured the first step might be to decide what we really our expect of our people, their performance, their attendance, and so on."

"But don't people know that already?" Marilyn asked. "We tell them when to get here, when to go on break, when to come back, where to stand, what the rules are – they know what's expected."

"Two problems I see with that," said Marty. "One: we shouldn't have to tell people where to stand, what to think, when to do every little thing if we really have high expectations and treat people like adults. Two: our rules actually communicate something different than our real expectations in some cases."

"So, you want to change policies?" Marilyn offered. This was something concrete she could deal with.

"Maybe, but there's more," Marty responded intensely. "Don't you see? | Policies should support high expectations

We can change policies all we want, and it won't solve anything. We have to set expectations and develop accountabilities. The policies *must support* our expectations. We have to set them and communicate them; ask people to make and keep commitments."

"Look, Marty, I really want to help, and I can see you're really passionate about it. If you want to change policies, we'll have to get corporate approval. It won't be easy. My advice is, if you see something else that needs to be done – defining expectations, talking with your people or whatever – just do it. But first you need to *clearly* identify what's wrong."

> Identify negatives that frustrate the 95%.

"You mean, identify the negatives; those things that really hold our good people back?"

"Yeah, I guess so. Where's the biggest hurt?" said Marilyn.

"That's easy: Attendance," Marty said. "Every week, one of our 95-%ers will complain to me about a 5-%er's absences."

Marilyn sank back into her chair. "Not *that* again," she said. "It's hopeless! We've tried point systems, no-fault systems, point*less* systems. Nothing works."

"Nothing we've *tried* works," corrected Marty. "What did all those systems have in common? We told people how much they could get away with before they were in trouble. And guess what? They lived *down* to our expectations."

"What we need is a fresh approach; one that says, 'We expect you to be here every day, on time, and we'll deal with abuses right away.' After all, Marilyn, how many of our people have a real, habitual attendance problem?"

"I don't know, but that would be easy to find," she said. "I can get Payroll to plot absences by employee for the last year. Tardies and early outs, too."

> Establish your baselines to measure against.

"My guess is, it's a handful of people with a serious pattern of problems, year after year. Their behavior leads others to believe it doesn't matter as long as you're inside the lines. The expectation becomes confused."

Marilyn began hesitantly. "Listen, Marty, I can work on the data..."

"...and I can work on drafting a new expectation," Marty interjected.

"... *but* you still have to figure out how to communicate that expectation. Especially how to ask people to commit to it," she concluded.

"We have to get them to see the consequences, like Bubba said," Marty muttered. "Not just what we expect, but why it's important to us and to them. It's how we approach it."

"Improving attendance won't be easy," Marilyn resumed. "You might want to consider some other 'negatives' to tackle first."

> Plan the important changes but start small – create a win!

"Yeah; suppose you're right. I've started my list already. There are plenty of little things that irritate people because they communicate 'We don't trust you'. We don't have to say it in words; our policies and actions give it away."

"Marty, aren't you afraid of losing control and making things worse?" Marilyn asked.

"Maybe, but think about it: Sure, a new approach may cause some pain, but how much hidden pain does our current approach cause? Turnover, morale, lost production, increased benefit costs, bad quality, scrap; you name it," he replied. "I don't know all the 'how' yet, but I think I see the 'what' and definitely the 'why'."

"Hey, if a few changes can improve all that, I'm behind you," she said. *"Way, way behind you,"* she thought.

14

A few days later, anyone walking by the window in Marty's office would think that Sonny had flipped – wildly gesturing as he paced back and forth in front of Marty's desk, his mouth flapping with his face pointed downward, eyes wide.

"How do you expect me to control production with a fool idea like this?" Sonny asked in amazement. "I can't keep some folks on the job *now*. With this, I'll have no idea who's supposed to be where!"

"You don't have to know," said Marty, calmly watching the production supervisor, "because the people know. Let me ask you: Did you have trouble with people coming back late from breaks and lunch before?"

"Of course I do," Sonny flapped, still pacing.

"So, if we tell people we expect them to take a 10-minute break sometime during the first and last half of their shift, and a 30 minute lunch at mid-shift, and eliminate the buzzer, do you think most people will be late? Or will it be the same ones?"

Sonny stopped in his tracks. He had to think about that. "Well, probably the same ones as now."

"And what does this practice say to the ones who are always back on time?" Marty asked.

"I guess that we expect them to do what they always done: be there on time to do a job."

> Seek buy-in, explain reasons; but don't wait for total agreement.

"And that we *trust* them to do that job, like they always have. It's a little thing, but little things mean a lot when you're trying to change. Things like cleaning the break room and painting the bathroom. I want to get some folks working on that after lunch," Marty said. "Let's go." Marty strode out the office door, Sonny right behind.

"And Sonny," Marty added as they walked, "what do you think about eliminating the requirement to work the day before and day after a holiday to get paid for the holiday? It's the same principle: Only a few people abuse it, and if we communicate it right, we can gain a lot of trust with the people who'd be here anyway . . ."

"*Oh, no, not another change*" Sonny thought as he scurried to catch Marty on his way to the employee meeting. "I think you might want to bake that one a little longer."

15

"Marty," came a soft voice from the hallway outside Marty's office

"Oh, come in, Missy. What's up?"

"I just wanted to tell you that several of us was talkin', and we think it's a good idea, lettin' us decide our own breaks. And, well, we appreciate what you said about the majority of us have proved we're responsible, and you expect us to keep that up. That means something."

Respect builds trust

"Thanks, Missy," Marty said, "but you know, it wasn't exactly a great stride for humanity. Lots of other companies let employees decide on their own break times. I figure if you're old enough to work, you can tell time. It won't hurt production, since we shut down all the machines anyway at break. Might even help it a little. And we do expect everybody to take *only* 10 minutes, and we'll deal with those that don't. So, I appreciate the kind words, but I'm not sure I deserve 'em."

"I ain't sure you do either," she laughed, "but it's not just that. Seems like you're trying to think about the workers a little more. Like when you come over and told me how much improvement you could see in my quality, and how important that was to you. That wasn't much, either, but I appreciated it. I figured nobody else would say nothing to you, so I decided to. 'Sides, if it was anybody *but* me the others might think I was kissing up to you. See you in the morning," she waved.

"Missy, hold on a second," he called. "I'd like to ask you to think about something for me."

"OK," she said cautiously.

"I've been thinking about a different way of dealing

with attendance. Some way that lets people know that we expect them here every day, on time, giving their best efforts. And that if they have good attendance regularly, they won't be in trouble if they miss a day, but if they have a pattern of missing work, they might be."

"Yeah," she said warily, "and what do you want me to do?"

"I just can't get the details down on paper as clearly as I'd like. I was thinking about having a small group to take a look at it and recommend to me what the policy and procedure should be." Do you think if we requested employees to volunteer to work on such a group people would do it? Would you consider volunteering?"

> Leaders set the direction and involve people.

"Marty, I don't know nothin' about writing policies," Missy objected, "and I ain't sure I want to be on *your* team; no offense. I might catch a lot of grief on the floor."

"Yeah, but you and the others would also be helping us turn a major corner. Attendance is a big problem for us. And I'd want a good cross-section of people, people with several different points of view on the team. A Supervisor, people with a history of good attendance, and maybe," he hesitated, ". . . some with *experience* with our current system. Four to six people. It can't be just 'my team'. It's important to all of us."

"Can I let you know tomorrow?" said Missy.

"Sure. See you tomorrow, then."

16

Returning to light duty had been good for Junior. His

friends at work really seemed glad to have him back. Dottie had been kind enough to bring dinner to his trailer several times since the wreck.

"Dottie, could you hand me a beer while you're puttin' the food out?" Junior asked.

"No. I'll fix you a glass of tea."

He started to complain but thought better of insulting his meal ticket.

"You aren't drinking while you're taking your medicine, are you?" she interrogated.

Caustically, he quipped, "Even I know better than that."

"Junior!"

"I'm sorry, I just get tired of hearing about my 'drinkin' problem'."

Dottie came over and sat on the couch across from Junior's threadbare easy chair. The place was filthy, decorated in old beer cans and dusty furniture. A picture of Junior's kids hung over the fireplace. Other snapshots of their family when Carol was around were scattered on the wall. A chilling wave of sadness passed through the room.

"I'm sure you do, Junior," she said, "but face it; You *do* have a problem. You drink too much sometimes. But that doesn't make you a bad person."

"It don't?" he replied doubtfully. "Then why do I feel so bad about ... everything?"

"Because some of your actions had bad results. You and Carol split up because of your drinking. That hurts," she said. "You had a wreck, messed up your arm and your car because of drinking. Your drinking's getting awful expensive. But you're not a 'problem person', you're a person with a problem."

"What's the difference, Dottie?" he shot back. "I'm still screwed up, ain't I?"

> To create change, focus on specific behaviors.

"The difference is, problems can be solved," she said firmly. "We're talking about behaviors – things you say or do — and those can be changed if you'll take action, get some help. Your feelings about yourself, your attitudes toward yourself and others: those will take longer. But you can start changing behaviors right now."

"Why should I?" Junior whined. "Carol ain't comin' back; she's married again. Kids are almost grown. I'm middle-age, broke, laid up and livin' in a dump. What's the point?"

A soft rap came at the screen door, echoed by loud bangs as the rickety metal door hit its facing. "Junior? Dottie, is that your car? Are y'all eatin' supper?"

"*Think* about it. You can change behaviors. All it takes is for you to make the effort," said Dottie, rising to let Missy in. "A lot of people will be there for you, Junior. It's worth it."

> **GREAT EXPECTATIONS**
> - **Define what you want to be different.**
> - **Start with negative that frustrate the 95%.**
> - **Plan big but start small.**

To Do List

- ☐ Ask one of your 95% employees for their ideas on solving a workplace issue, process, logistics, equipment, workflow, etc.
- ☐ Or Form a team to look at a specific problem and recommend solutions
- ☐
- ☐
- ☐

GREAT EXPECTATIONS

*Leaders have to set the direction and ask
for buy-in from their people.*

****

*"Workers are people too.
They'd like to be proud of where they
spend most of their time." – Bubba*

17

" . . . so I thought I'd start out our team meeting by asking each of you what your expectations are from this work we're doing on attendance," Marty said.

"That's easy," said Chuck flippantly. "I expect to get paid to sit here and yap for an hour. Then you'll do just what you want to anyway."

"Well, I expect us to think of some way to get some folks who can't get to work on time out the door," said Bubba, glaring at Chuck.

"Yeah; come on, Chuck," said Henry. "The least you can do is take this halfway serious. After all you did volunteer to *work* on this team. With folks absent, it really puts a load on the rest of us. We need to do something."

The work group on attendance hadn't started out exactly like Marty planned, but it seemed there were at least some feelings on the subject.

"I just don't see why we have to talk about it. They ain't gonna change the policy, and what we got's just fine," said Chuck. "Everybody knows what's expected."

Clarify expectations

"OK, Chuck, what *is* our expectation on attendance?" Marty quizzed.

Chuck paused a second. "Not to get no more points than the policy allows. Ain't it?"

"I think you're right on the money; that's what our current policy says," said Marty. "But guys, is that working?"

"Well, it's fair I reckon," said Missy, "cause everybody gets treated the same."

> "To treat everybody fairly, you have to treat everybody differently."
> - Ken Blanchard
> *The One Minute Manager*

"I don't know, Missy," said Henry. "First, I don't think everybody really gets treated the same. And second, even if they were, 'the same' ain't necessarily fair."

"How'd you mean, Henry?" asked Missy.

"Don't you see some folks who miss a lot, and keep on missing, and nothing ever gets done?" he replied.

"Wait, now, Henry," said Sonny, "I write up each and every person who's over the limit."

"And get 'em to do *what* exactly? I'll tell you what: nothing. And that's what changes – nothing!"

"Wait a minute, guys," said Marty, writing furiously on a flipchart. "We're actually making progress. First, we're identifying what's wrong with our current system. Chuck says it's OK now, and Missy says the current system is equal. Henry said he thinks its *un*fair

> Overcome obstacles through two-way communication.

to the people who are here all the time. It treats every situation alike. And there's no change in behavior."

Define specific behaviors

"What's this behavior stuff, anyway?" said Bubba.

"Well, attendance is a behavior; something tangible a person does that you can see or hear. How can you tell if someone has met the attendance expectation?"

"Well, you'd see 'em here!" Bubba replied.

"How often would you see them here?" said Marty.

"Well, every day."

"Even on Sunday?"

"Of course not – every day they're scheduled to be here," Bubba said.

"So the expectation for attendance really should be, 'Here every day, as scheduled'. That's a behavior you can describe, see, and track. Are they or aren't they? Yes or no. Now, when should they be here?"

"On time," said Henry, glaring at Chuck, "and that means back from lunch and breaks on time, too."

Chuck looked down at his pencil and silently mocked Henry's 'back from lunch and breaks on time, too!' with lips and eyes. His hand rose slightly from the table, fingers except the middle curling slightly, preparing to flash the 'bird' but stopping before it was fully in flight. Henry continued to stare angrily.

Marty chose to ignore the action unless it became disruptive. "Now explain to me what 'on time' means here, Missy?"

"I reckon it means at your workstation, ready to start work. But we really can't do that since we can't clock in no more than 7 minutes before start time?"

Marty hadn't thought about this contradiction. He wrote: *Conflict between clock-in and 'at workstation'.*

"So, our real expectation about attendance should be, **'Every day, on time, as scheduled'**, is that right?" Everyone except Chuck and Sonny nodded. "Sonny, you have a different thought?"

"Well, don't we need some way of measuring it? A number or something?" Sonny asked uncomfortably. "How will we know if somebody's in trouble?"

"Yeah, that's right," Chuck echoed. "We have a right to know when we'll be in trouble."

"Well, what's that number? How many days should a person miss a year?" Marty asked

"About 12; one a month," Chuck joked. No one laughed.

"Naw, be serious," Sonny chided. "I don't know, but we need to think about it."

"OK, but we need to know how many you're going to miss if we've got to draw a line," Bubba said. "Is it reasonable that somebody could go a week without missin'?"

Henry chortled for the first time. "Not for some folks!" The rest chuckled.

"Come on, Henry. Well, Sonny, is it reasonable?" Bubba persisted.

"Sure, I think most everybody could go a week without missing, under normal circumstances," said Sonny.

"How about two weeks?"

"Yeah."

"A month?"

Sonny looked around at the others as if seeking their thoughts. "Yeah, I guess a month is pretty fair."

"How about 3 months?"

"Now, I don't know about that. Folks get sick sometimes. Three months without an absence can be done, but not everybody can do it."

"So then missin' 4 days a year should be the limit?" Bubba was obviously driving at something.

Marty jumped in. "So, if that's the line – let's say it's 5 days — what happens when you cross it? We have to do something to you, right?" Sonny was staring, bewildered. "Can you tell me right now how many days you'll need to miss next year?"

"Well, hold on, boss-man," said Chuck, "That dog won't hunt. There's good and bad reasons to miss, right?"

"OK. If that's true, it's our job to agree on all of 'em,"

Bubba said. "Let's start the list."

Fifteen minutes later, Marty had two pages of reasons listed. Henry threw his pencil on the table and muttered an expletive.

"What's wrong, Henry?" Marty said.

"This is *stupid*. We've been arguin' for half an hour, and we ain't agreed on *nothin'*. You can't come up with a complete list of every reason somebody might need to miss work, and if you did, the jerks would just lie and use 'em anyway." He glared at Chuck, again.

"And that's my point," Marty said. "It's useless to define a specific point at which somebody's in trouble, or to list all the good and bad reasons somebody might need to miss. We can't do it in a way that's realistic and fair. Which brings us back to the expectation: 'Every day, on time, as scheduled'."

Bubba and the others nodded. Even Chuck didn't have any objection. But Bubba had a question: "Do we really expect *everybody* here absolutely *every* day?"

"That's our expectation for any one person, but realize that occasionally somebody may have to be out. Across the whole plant, we can't get to 'zero absences' forever, but we should still expect that you, and me, as *individuals* are to be here every day."

"So how do you get somebody to improve their attendance?" Bubba asked.

"By talking to people about expectations and commitments." Marty said.

Empowerment Made Easy
By William Byham
Author of *Zapp! The Lightening of Empowerment*

If a company wants to empower its workers, it should begin by removing stifling regulations, polices, and procedures – by asking employees what they think, listening to their answers, and acting on their suggestions. And most importantly, by giving workers increased responsibility and authority over a defined area that they can "own."

Empowerment means treating employees as "knowledgeable adults." To give workers more responsibility, managers need more than an intellectual understanding of what needs to be done. We have identified four key empowerment behaviors that need to be taught and practiced. They are:
- Maintain or enhance self-esteem
- Listen and respond with empathy
- Ask for help and encourage involvement
- Offer help without removing responsibility for action

Training is essential, and there needs to be a variety of things included. Managers need to be taught how to encourage and support initiative, to be coaches, and to provide feedback.

18

"So, you and Junior started seein' each other?" Bubba teased Missy after the meeting. "Dot told me you stopped by his place"

"Now, just listen here, Bubba Self," she launched in, "I'll see who I please, when I please, and it ain't none of your business."

He laughed. "You know I'm just teasin'. I really appreciate you stopping by there.

"I was glad too," Missy said. "But that place is a wreck if ever I seen one. Looks like a cave more than a trailer."

"He just needs a little training, that's all. And a little incentive. All by himself, he hasn't seen much of a point in tidying up the place."

Suddenly a sort of shrill, exaggerated smacking sound interrupted; a mock kiss. They eyed each other, then looked in unison at the source of the sound: Chuck.

"What's the matter; your lips locked up on you?" Bubba asked him.

Missy came nose to nose with Chuck. "And just what was *that* supposed to mean?"

"Well, nothing," he said, a little taken aback by her intensity, then settling into his bad-boy role, "except your lips might be a little chapped after kissin' up to Marty in there.

> When people attempt to change, they face pressure to revert.

"I ain't kissin' up to him *or* to you," she said, "but let me ask you something Chuck. Just why do you think Marty asked us to work on the team?"

"Like I said: to flap our jaws and get out of work for awhile, so he could do what he wanted to anyway."

"Is that what you think? Let me tell you what I think, Chuck; we were there because Marty wanted to know what we thought. He's giving you credit for having a brain, not just a mouth. You, and me, and all the rest of us are here to give it our best every day so we can keep our jobs."

"I'm giving these SOBs more than they deserve," Chuck said defiantly.

"You've been listening to Jimmy too long, Chuck. I think you're better than that. And I think you can give better than you've been giving. What do you think?"

"I think you better talk to somebody who cares," he said in parting.

Missy turned to Bubba, who was too shocked to move. "I guess I shoulda just ignored him," she said. But since I started seein' the reason I should care more about work, I just can't stand folks shootin' off their mouths like that. It's time the rest of us spoke up.

GREAT EXPECTATIONS

- **Leaders set the direction and engage and involve people.**
- **Build the buy-in of people who want to make things better, but don't wait for total agreement.**
- **95% employees can and will confront 5% behavior.**

To Do List

- ☐ Ask one of your 95% employees for their ideas on solving a workplace issue, process, logistics, equipment, workflow, etc.
- ☐ Or Form a team to look at a specific problem and recommend solutions
- ☐
- ☐
- ☐

TAKING IT PERSONALLY

You build trust by doing what's right, one encounter at a time.

****

"*If you show me you care, I'll trust you. If
I trust you, I'll help you.*" – Bubba

19

Junior swallowed hard as he walked toward the Plant Manager's door. He'd been there many times as steward, usually representing a fellow employee with a problem. Now, it was his turn, and he felt alone and small.

He tapped lightly on the secretary's door frame. "Come on in, Junior. Mike's expecting you. Can I get you some coffee?"

"No, thanks Sharon," Junior replied. His hands were a little shaky, and he didn't want to spill it on himself.

"We all really missed you while you were out. Not that we want to see *too* much of you now!" she joked. "He's off the phone. Go right on in."

The office seemed small and smelled of stale cigarettes. Mike stood up from behind his aging metal desk and came around it. Junior winced a little as Mike's hand raised as if to clap him heartily on his sore shoulder; then, whether aborting a joke or suddenly remembering Junior's injury, the hand dived to shake instead.

"Hey, Junior!" Mike said. "Kinda unusual to see you

here by yourself, ain't it?"

"Well," Junior's voice lowered, "I got something kinda personal to talk about."

"Oh," Mike replied more seriously, quietly pushing the door shut as he motioned to a couple of side chairs, "sit down and tell me what's up?"

Mike had been a good manager since arriving two years ago. Far from being the hard-nosed, union-busting type they had expected, he really seemed to know how to work together with the union leaders. They'd had some differences, but Mike knew how to give and take. All Junior and the committee had asked was fairness, and Mike gave that. But after seeing him as an adversary – even if a friendly one – for so long, it was awkward to be here.

"I need some help, Mike," Junior said. "Since the accident, I sort of began to think."

"Yeah, that 'life passing before your eyes' stuff really happens, doesn't it?" Mike said, trying to lighten the mood.

"Well, not exactly. See, I know that . . . well, sometimes I drink too much. Never at work, now, you understand," he added quickly, "but after work. And, you know, I kinda think it's time . . . I don't know how, but . . ." Junior looked up into Mike's eyes for the first time.

"You want some help dealing with alcohol abuse, Junior?" Mike asked gently.

"Yes, sir, I do," he said. "I need some. I didn't really know who to talk to, and . . ."

"I'm glad you felt like you could talk to me about this, Junior," Mike said. "That means a lot to me."

"Well, we've been through a lot together. You ain't

roasted anybody that didn't deserve it yet, and I was countin' on not bein' the first one."

"Well, that's how you build trust: doing what's right, one encounter at a time," Mike said. "I know you'd help me, too. Now, let's talk about how to get started..."

20

"Getting people to be accountable, that's the key" Marty thought as he carried his tray from the steak house serving line to the banquet room. These monthly Chamber of Commerce operations forums weren't often useful, but it did give him a chance to see other plant managers.

Active listening

As Marty sat down the manager of the plant where Junior worked came in. "Have a seat, Mike," Marty called.

"Thanks, I will. How's things going?" Mike asked.

"Pretty well," he muttered without changing his pose.

"So, what were you thinkin' so hard about?"

Marty looked surprised, but. Mike had always been insightful. That was one of the things Marty liked about him. Mike really paid attention to people and seemed to know what to say.

"How'd you know that I was thinking about something?"

Mike grinned. "I'd like to say it was my natural powers of perception, but it isn't. We had some training in active listening for our managers, and body language is part of that. Now, you have

> Body Language

to be careful not to read too much between the lines, but it can sorta tell you if someone's tense, or worried, or angry or upset. You know; whether to talk or run."

"Active listening? What exactly is "active" about it?" Marty was clearly interested.

"Active listening is the most important tool a leader can have," Mike extolled. "See, most of our listening is passive. We just sit there. Active listening keeps both people engaged in the process by asking open-ended questions."

> Open-ended Questions

"What do you mean by open-ended questions? Marty asked.

"Open-ended questions can't be answered with a simple 'yes' or 'no'."

"How does that help you listen?"

"Real simple," Mike said, finishing his first bite. "It helps you get the other person talking. Gives you information that you'd miss if you were doing all the talking. Open-ended questions can only start with certain words that can start open-ended questions: who, what, when, where, why, how."

"But don't people sometimes avoid answering?" Marty quizzed.

Sure. But you just make comfortable eye contact and wait for the answer. Resist the urge to jump in when it's quiet. Maybe use body language like nodding your head or turning an open palm to give them a cue that you're waiting."

So after they answer, then what?"

"Well, it depends on what they say. Many times, you restate what you heard them saying. You don't just repeat it verbatim but summarize what their main point was. You can say, 'I want to make sure I understand,' then summarize. Checks for your understanding and gives them a chance to add stuff."

> Restatement

"How do you know when somebody's not telling the whole story?" Marty asked.

"You don't, but you can get an idea by watching their body language and listening to their tone of voice, their pitch and speed," Mike replied. "And there's a place for 'yes or no' questions, too. Like to clarify details of a story, or contradictions. 'Did you mean it happened like this, or was it like that?'"

> Listen for Total Meaning

Marty thought about Sonny, and others in a leadership role at the plant. "This sounds tough to do. Did your supervisors really take to it, even in a union shop?"

"Yeah, and we trained the stewards, too. They ought to know how to listen actively. See, most people don't like to just out-and-out lie to you, but if you don't ask the right question, they don't feel the need to volunteer much. Active listening really helps make them more accountable for their behaviors. And it keeps you from guessing what really went on." "Plus, it builds mutual understanding of what caused the problem, and what's in it for the employee to fix it," Mike added.

Understanding before commitment

Marty thought, "I guess before you can get a commitment, you have to understand not only *what* happened, but what *causing* the problem. The other person has to understand *why* it's important, and what's *expected*. Active listening helps you get there. Then, you can get commitment to specific changes."

It was time for the speaker. "This guy's the one who taught our class," Mike whispered. Marty looked at the speaker's first slide to see the topic: "Active Listening Skills". *'Maybe these luncheons are useful after all,'* Marty thought.

21

"I'm gonna take you down, boy! I don't care if we both go, but I'm takin' you with me! Do you hear me?! I'm sick and tired of you thinkin' you can get by with just whatever flies into that pea brain of your'n, and they ain't payin' me enough to put up with the likes of you. Well? What you got to say, Jimmy?"

For a moment, Marty was frozen with shock at what he heard Sonny screaming from across the pack-out room.

Things had been going pretty well, he thought. Missy had shown Barb a new way of stacking finished parts that was easier and reduced damage. The attention seemed to soften Barb a little, and she hadn't missed or been late in nearly a month. Henry had been showing the new operator next to him some techniques he'd learned, and his usually gruff veneer was peeling away to reveal his good nature. Sonny had even been seen complimenting someone for hustling to expedite an order.

Now, this. He'd heard a commotion from his office, and by the time he tracked it to the back almost everyone had stopped to listen.

"OK, get on back to work, folks," Marty said matter-of-factly as he walked past them toward the source of the disruption. "Sonny, what's going on?" he said evenly.

"The same thing that's been going on for as long as I can remember: this goof-off, hare-brain nitwit has mixed up part numbers, again, an' he's givin' me lip about

WINNERS & LOSERS

As Einstein said, the definition of insanity is to do the same thing over and over and expect different results.

****

"If you always do what you've always done, you'll always get what you've always got." – Bubba

22

Jimmy shuffled his feet a bit, looking at the floor as he sat in Marty's office again. Sonny took the lead.

"First off, Jimmy, I apologize for losin' my cool out there. What you were doin' wasn't right, but the things I said wasn't right either."

Jimmy hesitated, looking first at Sonny and then at Marty for cues as to whether the time was right for an attack. He sensed it should wait. "All right," Jimmy said noncommittally. "Is that all?" He started to rise.

"No Jimmy, it ain't," Sonny said, irritation flashing in his eyes. Marty looked at him, wondering if he should take over. Sonny continued evenly. "The situation where I lost my temper all got started because of your performance today. Here's a disciplinary action report for you to read and sign." Sonny slid the paper across the corner of the desk. "It says that you're being wrote up because you packed parts improperly and mixed 'em up in a box, and that you was insubordinate in the way you talked to a supervisor. You got any comments?"

Jimmy pushed the paper back across the desk, sunk back in his chair and folded his arms across his chest. "No, but it ain't fair. I was just doin' what y'all said you wanted. I reckon it don't pay to think around here. I won't never pack different parts in the same box again, no matter what." There was just a hint of smirk in Jimmy's expression, leading Marty to wonder what he meant by, *"no matter what."*

"All right, just sign the form and we'll be done," Sonny said.

"I ain't signin' nothin', cause it ain't fair," Jimmy replied.

"Jimmy," Marty chimed in, "signing it doesn't mean you're agreeing with us, just that you received a copy of the form."

"I know the drill, Mr. Peoples, I got plenty of them." Jimmy said, "but I still ain't signing."

"Employee refused to sign" Sonny scrawled, sliding it across to Marty. "Marty, if you'll witness that Jimmy refused to sign, we'll give him his copy. Now, Jimmy," he turned, "this is your first written warning for this offense, and like it says, if you pull anything like this again it could . . ."

". . . lead to further disciplinary action, up to and including termination, blah-blah," Jimmy completed sarcastically. "Yeah, like I said, I know the drill."

"Jimmy, we're giving you some consideration here," Marty replied, "and it would be in your best interests to show more cooperation. We're talking about your employment."

"Here's your copy," Sonny said, ripping the back page of the form off and handing it to Jimmy. "I expect you to follow procedures in the future, and to talk more respectful."

"I reckon I will if you will," Jimmy said, rising. "Can I go back to work now?"

23

Bubba laughed as he recounted Jimmy's version of the story he heard in the breakroom.

"Yeah, Jimmy was talking just like ol' Arnold what's-his-name in The Terminator; 'I'll be back,'" Bubba impersonated to Marty and Marilyn, here for her regular visit.

"I'm sure he will, Bubba," Marty said resignedly. "That's the problem. We can tell people what we expect in terms of performance and attendance," Marty said, "but the problem comes when someone doesn't meet the expectation. Just giving out write-ups and suspensions doesn't work, especially to folks like Jimmy. But can *anything* work?"

"Well," Bubba replied, stroking his chin as he thought, "first off, what exactly do you want to happen when you talk with 'em about their attendance, or any kind of performance problem?"

"That's kind of obvious, isn't it?" Marty said. "We want them to stop doing the wrong things, and start doing the right ones." Marilyn nodded, a bit amused at the strategy discussion between a plant manager and a set-up technician.

"Really?" said Bubba, grinning. "I thought the point was to get rid of 'em."

"Well, sometimes that happens, but we don't want it – I guess," Marty said, unsure.

Bubba chuckled. He liked rattling Marty's cage just a bit; making him think. "I wouldn't be too sure, now. If you read your policy, it looks like you *really* plan to fire 'em."

Marty saw his point. Something had always made him uncomfortable with treating people worse and worse in the hope they'd behave better and better. The fear that the real intent was to fire people made supervisors avoid addressing problems until it was almost too late – or simply yell, scream and swear instead of using the process. Like Sonny.

"And the stupid thing is, it don't do much good, anyway," Bubba continued. "The ones you want to fire can play the game, and the ones you ought to help just get tore up about it."

"Like Jimmy who's constantly skating on the edge, and Sam who got punished for an honest mistake," Marty thought. Their discipline system, like most, consisted of the familiar one-page, pre-printed form for 'write-ups', filled out before the employee came in – except, of course, for the 1 inch "employee comments" section which they usually either left blank or filled with unmentionable terms. The 'read it

and sign it' process took about five minutes; and the results didn't even last *that* long. There was almost no discussion of why the problem occurred, or any commitment to change behaviors.

Another problem was that each disciplinary action was only for one or two specific behaviors, not for a pattern of misbehavior. That's what Jimmy had meant by saying, "*I won't pack* **those** *parts together, no matter what.*" He intended a kind of 'malicious obedience' changing only the specific behavior defined on the disciplinary form.

And, of course, if the employee could avoid that specific violation for a certain length of time, he got to repeat the step the next time. No wonder the jerks called the forms 'toilet paper'. Still, the system was legal, and the forms provided documentation. And, frankly, he'd never heard of anything different. Marty glanced at Marilyn.

"You know what I think: we need to start over," said Bubba.

"Well, what would you suggest?" Marilyn asked.

"That's the problem. I don't know what to do differently. I just knowwhat we have doesn't work," said Marty.

"Well, when you're talking to sombody about a problem, what's the first ting you want to make sure of?" MArilyn asked.

Marty thought about the change process, "First, we have to make sure they're aware of the problem – what the expectation is, and how their actions differ from that."

> Make expectations clear and seek the employee's agreement.

"Yep, you're right. Most folks know what's expected, but some might not. How you gonna do that?"

> Use performance counseling to build personal accountability.

"Obviously, talk to them one-on-one. Ask them what they believe the expectation is, and how they believe their behavior matches up. Clear up any misunderstandings and get their commitment to meet the expectation."

"So, would you write 'em up?"

Marty thought about it – did he really believe that *most* people wanted to do what's right?

"No," he finally said. "I don't think so."

> Document informal conversations.

"But, supervisors ought to make a note that the conversation occurred, maybe on their calendar or something, even if they put nothing in the file yet," Marilyn added prudently.

"OK, what next?"

Marty lightened up a bit. "Well, of course, the problem is solved!" Marilyn snickered.

"Maybe it is, smarty-pants, but what if they keep on screwin' up?" Bubba retorted.

"Well, you'd have to have flexibility based on the behaviors you see. Is the person trying and can't get it, or is the person obviously seeing how far he can push the system? I think you have a second, more serious conversation with them," said Marty.

"Oh, so you're gonna talk 'em to death?" Bubba said.

> Find the reason behind the continuing failure

"No. This second conversation focuses on why they didn't keep their commitments. This is much more serious than the first one, because if they don't keep their commitments, trust has been broken," Marty explained. "This time, you document. But that form doesn't seem like the right way to do it."

Marilyn looked around. In Marty's in-box, she could see a couple of memos from corporate. That gave her an idea. "Marty, think about it – when there's been a problem involving a couple of managers, how do they keep a record of who agreed to what?"

> Use a memo to outline the problem behaviors, new behaviors expected, and the employee's commitment to change.

"A memo," Marty said, catching her train, "summarizing what was said, and who agreed to do what. Instead of a form, we should just write a summary memo *after* the meeting. Put in it what the employee said, and what they agreed to do. And," he added, "explaining that this can't continue without sustained improvement. You have to let them know that this is very serious, and that they could lose their job."

"So, what you're really doing at this point is recording their commitment." Marilyn said.

"More than that. We're really developing commitment and a plan to achieve a new level, not just clarifying the expectation like we were the first time. And documenting it, too," Marty said.

"So let's say that don't solve the problem," Bubba proposed. "How long do you keep a jawin' about it?"

"Not long," said Marty. "You shouldn't repeat this

process just because a certain number of days has passed. You spend enough time at each phase to develop a commitment; you don't stop until you have one. Once a person makes a commitment, they're accountable for it. If they don't live up to it, you move forward. After the second conversation, I think you have one more chance in most cases. That's it."

> Hold people accountable for the commitments they make.

"But it would depend on the situation, wouldn't it?" asked Bubba.

"Sure. Bubba, there are clearly some things you should be fired for right away..." Marilyn said.

"I didn't do nothin'!" Bubba said in mock surprise.

"Not you *personally*," Marty replied, pointing his finger, "though I could probably find something if I thought about it. You know what I mean: violence, theft, sleeping on the job. Those things should bypass the early conversations and go straight to termination."

"But don't you need leeway for a little judgment even in those?" Bubba asked.

"You still have to listen to the person and get the facts. Talk to witnesses," said Marilyn.

"Right. You need flexibility to start at any phase," said Marty, "but those situations will be rare. We should expect that most problems will be solved after one conversation. Some will require two. And if there isn't lasting improvement, we should have one final attempt."

"Kind of sayin', 'We can't go on like this,'" Bubba said. "This is the point where you have to decide if you want to keep your job."

"And the company has to decide if we really have any reason to believe you'll improve," said Marty. "We ought to ask people to go home and think about it."

> Give one last chance.

"Whatcha mean, 'Think'?" Bubba asked. "It wouldn't take me long to decide that."

"Yes, but legally we have to give people due process," said Marilyn. "It's not right to ask them to decide on the spot." We need to suspend them for a day or two so they can think about it.

"Hold on Marilyn! Do suspensions really work? Marty quizzed. "And besides, isn't telling an employee they can't come to work contradictory to our attendance expectations? Wouldn't we be sending mixed signals? Especially if the issue is attendance?

"I get it" Bubba replied. I guess it would be good to have some time to cool off or calm down and think about it. I think if a person cares, overnight should be enough time."

> Require a personal plan for change.

"And when they come back the next shift, they need to bring a plan for how they will improve their attendance, or quality, or production, or whatever it is," said Marty.

"So we can sorta see if they're takin' it serious?" Bubba said. "Yeah, I like that. But some folks can't hardly write their name, much less a plan."

"The writing's not important; the plan is," Marty said. "We can help them write it down, but they have to think it through and commit to it. Remember, Bubba, at this phase we're at the end of the trail. We've already had at least two detailed conversations with them except in rare situations. We can help, but it has to be their commitment."

"So what if they come in and say, 'Tell me what to do, boss, and I'll do it'?" Bubba said.

Marty shook his head. "Not good enough. We need for them to take some responsibility for the problem."

Firing with respect

"So if they don't improve after this, or if they won't come up with a plan you can buy, they're fired, right?" said Bubba.

"Yes. And we don't want to kick them while they're down. No screaming. We need to be as professional and respectful when they're leaving as when they came," said Marty.

"Maybe you should offer 'em a chance to resign."

Marilyn nodded agreement. "Yes, if it's for ongoing performance, we should let them resign. It's called a requested resignation. On the other hand, if it's for gross misconduct like theft or violence, we should not give them that option."

They both paused. It seemed too simple as Marty made notes in his daybook:

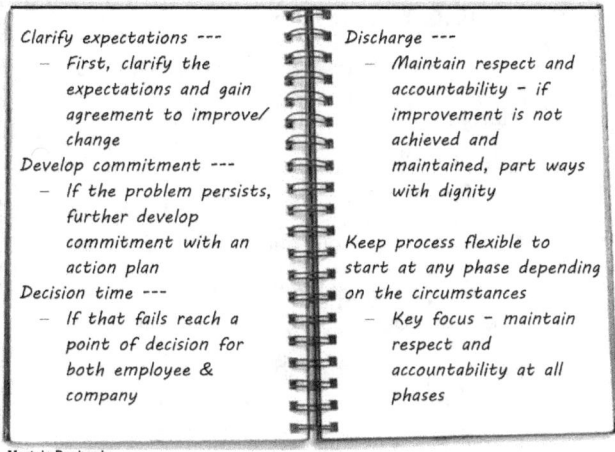

Marty's Daybook

"Guys, can this work? If it's really this simple, why isn't everybody doing it?"

"I reckon some people are. You just never hear about 'em, cause they ain't in a uproar all the time," said Bubba.

"Sure, Bubba," said Marilyn, "they expect people to do right, and for the most part they do. They don't have a lot of problems, because they expect people to have *self-discipline*."

"And they don't take 15 years to fire somebody who ain't puttin' forth the effort, either. See, they've figured out what winning really is," Bubba continued. "It ain't beating the other guy; it's beating the problems *with* the other guy. **Respect** is what **winning** is all about."

REDESIGNING THE SYSTEM

- Identify negatives which frustrate the 95%
- Plan important changes but start small.
- Seek buy-in, explain the reasons, but don't wait for total agreement.
- Leaders set the direction and involve people.
- Overcome obstacles through two-way communication using active listening.
- Leaders "win" when they show respect; "lose" when they violate a person's dignity.
- Use a performance counseling process to develop personal accountability.

To Do List

☐ Examine your discipline or corrective action policy. What's its real focus: problem solving and commitment or creating a paper trail?

☐ If it needs work, think about the change process. How can you create awareness, understanding and commitment among those who must improve?

☐
☐
☐

ENSURING ACCOUNTABILITY

Treating people with Respect means expecting them to act like adults –
and confronting problems immediately and directly.

****

Seems if people give better, they
oughta get better – Bubba

24

Marilyn has told Marty to expect that the policy changes he wanted to make would not be warmly received. Still he wasn't prepared for the objections he heard from Tom, corporate Vice President of Human Resources, as they talked by phone.

"I understand it's different . . . but nothing else has worked," Marty said. "Marilyn thinks we should give it a chance."

"But with this approach, we'll be vulnerable to legal charges," Tom said.

"No more than we have been in the past," Marty reasoned. "The counseling process will require skills training for supervisors, but it provides due process and documentation."

"But from what I can see, only after the *second* step," Tom retorted. "It doesn't give enough repeated warnings. And we need to allow ourselves the option to suspend people."

"But Tom, we've been suspending people for years. The jerks see it as a vacation, and it's humiliating to the people who care. The main objection to suspensions is that they rarely work – especially when we're *suspending* people because they won't *come* to work."

"Humph," Tom replied, obviously unable to counter the logic. "Well, how will you ensure supervisors are consistent if there is no specified line that people cross before talking to them? We'll be overrun with complaints of favoritism."

"It's my job as manager to work with the supervisors to review attendance and performance records and make sure that people are being dealt with fairly," said Marty. "Tom, all I'm trying to do is create a system which sets a high expectation, and counsels with people to hold them accountable for their commitments. This kind of approach is new for us but has worked at other places."

"Yes, it's new for us, and quite frankly, it's a little too lenient," Tom said.

""How can it be lenient, when we don't define any certain amount of time that it's OK for people to miss?" Marty inquired. "If anything, it's *less* lenient. We as managers will have to record time missed and talk with people before problems become serious."

"Marty, people need to have a line; they need to know when they'll be in trouble," Tom said. Marty shook his head at the parallel between Tom's comment and Chuck's in the meeting. "Besides, we can't have one plant that's different from our other plants. It'll be chaos."

"But Tom, how can it be chaos for anyone but us? It's our responsibility."

"Have you talked with Frank about this? I can't believe he'd support such a risky change."

"Yes, I have talked with Frank in general, and I sent him this proposal at the same time I sent it to you. We haven't talked in detail yet. He wanted to get your views."

"Well, I'll call him to discuss it. I want us to take some time and think this through before rushing into it. In the meantime, just crack down on abusers using the policy you have. I guarantee you'll see improvement," Tom said.

"Yeah, for how long?" thought Marty.

"Besides, Marty, this is really a bad time to be talking about changing anything. We're preparing for compliance audits; we have depositions in several cases, and major benefits changes are coming up. I don't see how we can address this before next year."

> Change is always difficult; it's never the "right" time to change.

"If we're too busy to address problems, how will we ever get better?" thought Marty. "Well, let's get with Frank to see what we can work out. This is important to us. Thanks. Bye."

Bubba stood at the door, grinning. "So what are you looking at?" Marty snapped.

"Looks like you're yappin' with the big dogs," Bubba

said. "Who was that?"

"Tom, the VP of HR. He doesn't like the policy we drafted on attendance or the counseling process. Says it's too risky; it won't work; it isn't consistent with the other plants, it will cause favoritism, and on and on."

"It sure is easy to find reasons *not* to do something, ain't it?" Bubba said.

"I wish I could figure out what his *real* problem is," Marty said.

"Sort of like trying to get a bead on a hummin'bird from 500 yards," Bubba replied. "Hard to pin down. You know, a lot of it's just being afraid of a different idea, or bein' comfortable. Some's just bein' naturally cautious, wantin' to protect the company."

> Don't waste momentum trying to argue with hard-core skeptics. Let results speak for you.

"Yeah, it's easy to see what might go wrong with a new idea. I just wish he could see what's going wrong *now.*"

"Well, when I'm about to try something I ain't too sure about, I sorta like to have a 'trial run'; you know, a shakedown cruise, before I put it out for everybody to laugh at."

Marty stopped pacing. "That's a good idea, Bubba. We could be a pilot, a test case. Give us a certain amount of time; measure the before and after results and see how it works."

"I reckon the real question is, does the company really expect you be responsible for running this place, or are you just keepin' the chair warm for 'em?"

Marty believed he knew his boss Frank's answer to that. *"Now, time to see if Frank trusts me to get results,"* Marty thought as he picked up the phone.

25

Getting approval from Frank, Marty's immediate manager, for a pilot of the new attendance approach and counseling policy for performance problems wasn't too difficult. They had agreed on a target of 96% average daily attendance within 6 months – even though Tom thought it was impossible. "Now, to convince the employees," Marty thought as he prepared to roll it out.

Presenting the new plan

Several members of the attendance policy team spoke at the employee meeting to announce the change. "Now, I'm being honest," Bubba told the employees, "Not everybody on our team was entirely sold on this approach, especially at first. But we *were* in general agreement that we needed to do something about attendance, and that our previous point system and no-fault policies hadn't worked."

For a moment Bubba was afraid Chuck might disagree, but finally he nodded 'yes'. Jimmy and a couple of others stared at the floor as Missy and Henry gave the rationale for the change. Most of his audience sat with arms crossed, heads leaning slightly to one side, with mild skepticism on their faces.

Marty then outlined the basics of the policy: the attendance expectation was "every day, on time, as scheduled"; no set number of days it was OK to miss. Doctor's notes would no longer be required. Supervisors would record attendance on special calendars which allow them to spot patterns. Marty would meet with each supervisor monthly to review calendars and discuss any potential problems. Emphasis would be on direct, honest communication about absences. Call-in was still expected.

He then moved to the counseling policy. When it looked like a problem was developing, performance counseling would be used to discuss the cause and gain commitment to a solution. He explained the four phases; *Clarifying Expectations, Developing Commitment, Decision Making Time and Discharge.* Counseling would begin at whatever stage was appropriate based on the situation. Suspensions were eliminated, but termination could result if problems weren't fixed. People would be held accountable for their performance and their commitments. Marty's door was open for any concerns. And finally, all current disciplinary actions for attendance – and only for attendance – would be nullified. Everyone would start with a clean slate.

"I want to emphasize that the vast majority of people will not be impacted at all by this change," Marty concluded, "because the vast majority are here every day, on time, now. People who 'walked the line' in the past *will* see a difference. We'll meet with each of you over the next two weeks to discuss your situation and answer any questions."

There was a general buzz as people dispersed. Jimmy began lobbying. "You know what they're doin' this for, don't you," he said to Barb and Missy as they walked toward the door. "They're gonna get rid of us that's been here a long time and bring in cheaper labor."

"How they gonna do that, Jimmy?" Missy asked.

"Easy. They're gonna fire you if you miss a day. Didn't you hear him? *'Every* day, on time.' So Barb, if your baby's sick and you take him to the doctor, you'll get your pink slip."

"They couldn't do that, could they?" Barb asked Missy.

"Don't make much sense, does it?," Missy said. "But I'll talk to Marty to make sure."

As Missy left, Jimmy said to Barb, "Yeah, she'll go talk to Marty, but you wait and see who gets it first. It won't be his pets, I'll tell you that. I ain't waiting around to let them screw us."

26

Marty and the supervisors were holding one-on-one meetings with employees to discuss the new attendance policy and expectation. Although the purpose was to give special attention to people whose historical performance suggested they might have trouble meeting expectations, they had decided to start with a few "easy" employees. Sam was Marty's first. Marty was finding even Sam wasn't so easy, after all.

"How do we know the company won't take advantage of us?" Sam asked. Since his suspension, he was more suspicious of company actions than before.

"But your record on attendance is exemplary. I wish we had 100 like you," Marty said. "What do you mean when you say the company might 'take advantage of you', Sam?".

"Well, suppos'n I *was* to get sick; bad sick, like a heart attack," Sam said. "Wouldn't you kick me out the door?"

This sounded like Jimmy's work. In the two days since the meeting, he'd had his own one-on-ones with almost everyone, planting seeds of doubt about the intent and the impact.

"I understand your concern. But that would be foolish on our part; wouldn't it, Sam?" Marty said. "Why would we want to get rid of one of our best people?"

"Yeah, but there ain't any guarantee, is there?" Sam said. He was upset, and afraid. "The old way, at least we knew how far we had to go. This way, it's just whatever the boss says."

"No, Sam, it isn't," Marty said. "If you're afraid of losing your job when you get sick, remember that we got a leave policy and a disability policy, too. If you were seriously ill, you'd go on leave of absence. Then if you didn't get well enough to work, you'd receive disability. That's the same as it's always been. All we have done is take away the excuses and the lines that the 5 percent uses to play games."

"How will I know if I'm in trouble?" Sam asked, half convinced.

"Sam, you haven't ever *been* in trouble for attendance. Just look at your attendance calendar. Are you planning to start missing work now?" Marty teased.

"Now, you know I don't mean it that way," Sam retorted. "I always believed that a fair day's pay deserved a fair day's work, and I ain't plannin' to change now."

"And you've proved your commitment by your good

attendance, Sam," Marty said. "If you're sick, whether for a day or a long time, you won't be in trouble. Those who have a *pattern* of missing work will be in trouble. The supervisors will meet with Marty each month and go over attendance records, to keep track of the problems and to make sure we're fair."

> Even the 95% can fear change – so when people resist, build understanding through active listening.

"So, you ain't out to fire people?" Sam asked tentatively.

"No, unless someone's attendance pattern shows a *lack* of commitment to be here on time every scheduled day," Marty said. "Then we'll have to either see a change or part company with them."

Ensure Accountability

- Don't waste momentum trying to argue with hard-core skeptics. Let results speak for you.
- Even the 95% can fear change – so when people resist, build understanding through active listening.

MAKING A DIFFERENCE

Expect changes to be challenged . . . your response communicates your commitment.

****

Don't be surprised when people try ya." – Bubba

27

About a week after implementation of the new attendance expectation, Chuck and Jimmy were both absent on the same day, and neither called in to report the reason for the absence.

"Reckon I'm gonna have to grab some cables and jump-start them boys," Sonny said to Marty. "I don't care how you handle 'em, you can't change people like that."

Marty was disappointed in Chuck – and a little surprised. Next morning, Marty was near the employee entrance talking with folks. When Chuck arrived, his head hung down, and he tried to blend in with the group and go straight to his workstation.

"Missed you yesterday, Chuck," Marty called, then walked over. "Was anything wrong?"

Marty knew perfectly well where he'd been. Several employees had seen them at the Palace the night before.

> Remember – It's an employee with a problem **NOT** a problem employee.

Jimmy was really piling it on about Chuck's becoming

'Marty's boy'. Said they 'ought to lay out and go fishing.' Apparently, they did.

"No, sir," Chuck said awkwardly, his gaze still fixed on the ground. "Just a little under the weather, that's all." Marty mused that the sun on his face indicated the 'weather' he was 'under' must have been nice.

"What kept you from calling in?"

Chuck's eyes peeked up from under the brim of his cap. He could see that Marty wasn't angry, but maybe a little disappointed. "Uh, I just forgot, I guess." The silence seemed to Chuck to last for five minutes, though it couldn't have been more than a couple of seconds. Marty motioned for Chuck to come with him, and they talked as they walked.

"Chuck, you know that when we were establishing the attendance policy, we emphasized the importance of calling in, as well as being here every day. You remember?"

Chuck nodded. Marty observed that he looked like a kid on his way to the principal's office, so he stopped and turned toward Chuck. "Sonny's your supervisor, and he'll talk with you later today about your reason for not calling in, because that's a problem we can't ignore. But I just needed to ask you for my own satisfaction: Were you sick yesterday? Honest – just you and me."

"Marty, I've jerked you around a little, but I ain't never lied to you, and I ain't gonna start now," Chuck said. "No, I wasn't sick. I was fishin'. I didn't call in 'cause I wasn't gonna lie." Chuck's posture visibly straightened as he talked, like a weight was lifted off his back.

Stay calm and hold people accountable

"I appreciate that, Chuck. I didn't think you'd lie to me," Marty said. "You're not that kind of person. But how do you think what you did measures up to our expectation on attendance?"

> "When you have to reprimand, focus on the behavior, not the person. And let the individual know that you are disappointed."
> - Ken Blanchard
> *The One Minute Manager*

"Not good at all," Chuck said. "I shouldn't a done that. It was Jimmy's idea . . ." he halted in mid-excuse, "but I went along with it. You got my word, that's the last time I'll lay out 'less I'm bad sick or something. And if I have to be out, I'll call."

"I'm counting on that. You catch anything?" Marty asked, smiling.

"No, that's the worst part – all I caught is grief from you!" Chuck smiled.

Sure enough, after Sonny counseled both Chuck and Jimmy on their absence and failure to call in, Chuck's attendance was outstanding. Amazingly enough, Jimmy's attendance was perfect, too, for over a month – although he was still giving the minimum on the job.

One morning a few weeks later, Bubba stuck his head into the office about 15 minutes after start-up. "Y'all seen Chuck this morning?" he asked Sonny and Marty.

"No; come to think of it, I ain't," Sonny said. "His buddy Jimmy's back there if you need something."

Just then they heard the squeal of car tires turning too fast, then the crunch of gravel under wheels from the parking lot. Moments later, the employee door burst open, and Chuck came flying through. His shirttail was half in and half out; his hair (which was never too neat) sticking up randomly like a porcupine hit by lightning. He grabbed his timecard, slammed it in, and almost lept into Sonny's office. Bubba's wrinkled nose gave evidence that Chuck hadn't showered recently. All their mouths hung open, and Chuck's tongue hung out. He spoke before anyone had a chance.

"I'm sorry I'm late," Chuck said breathlessly. "My clock got cut off and I woke up 15 minutes ago. I come as fast as I could."

"Slow down, man," said Sonny, "and catch your breath. We just found out you was late."

"Well, I gave you and Marty both my word that I wouldn't be absent or late no more 'less it was a emergency," Chuck said, "and I don't like to break my word. I'll work over tonight to make it up if y'all will let me." Bubba excused himself.

"Have a seat just a minute and catch your breath before you go to work," Sonny said. As Chuck breathed deeply, Marty said, "Chuck, I appreciate your effort to let us know what's going on. It seems to me that you understand what our expectation is . . ."

"Yes, sir," Chuck panted, "every day, on time."

"And you know that you didn't meet that expectation today?"

"That's right."

"So, how are you going to make sure that this doesn't

become a pattern?"

Chuck's mouth twisted momentarily. "A pattern?"

"Other words, how you gonna keep this from happening over and over?" Sonny clarified. Marty was impressed.

> To deal with problem behaviors:
> - Ensure awareness of the problem and understanding of its importance.
> - Give them a chance to explain; listen actively and ask open-ended questions.
> - Ask for their commitment to a specific change.
> - Support good-faith tries even if they stumble.

"Oh, that's easy. Move the clock to where nobody can hit it by accident, tell my family not to touch it, and be sure to check it before bed," Chuck said. "I might even get me a battery clock in case the power goes out. My wife could use one, anyway."

"Chuck, I appreciate your commitment, and we expect you to live up to it. Please don't let this mess up the improvements you've made lately, OK?" Marty said.

28

Bubba figured trouble was brewing when he saw Jimmy hovering near Chuck right after the incident as the latter was trying to work. He figured he'd investigate and managed to find a machine adjustment that happened to be within earshot.

"... so what'd he say then?" Jimmy quizzed Chuck.

"Well, after I told him how I was gonna make sure I was on time in the future, Sonny just said he appreciated my commitment, he expected me to live up to it, and that he didn't want to see me mess up no more," Chuck replied.

"That's it? No write up or nothin'?" Jimmy said. "Cool."

Bubba ran into Sonny later. "You might keep your eye peeled for ol' Jimmy. I heard him pesterin' Chuck about what was said to him this mornin'."

"Are they plannin' some more foolishness?" Sonny asked.

"Naw, at least Chuck ain't. He told Jimmy he appreciated how you an' Marty treated him, and he wasn't gonna lie to nobody," Bubba said, "but that don't apply to Jimmy."

29

Sure enough, the next morning about 10 after, Jimmy wasn't at his workstation. He ambled in through the back entrance, whistling. He waved and spoke to a couple of people on his way to the time clock, punched in, and casually strolled back toward his area. Sonny intercepted him about halfway.

"Mornin' Jimmy. I noticed you was a little bit late this mornin'," Sonny said.

"Yeah, so?" Jimmy volleyed. "I ain't as late as Chuck was yesterday, and you didn't do nothin' to him. So you can't do nothin' to me."

"Jimmy, that ain't the point. You were late just now. I

ain't concerned about anybody's performance but yours."

"Oh, but see, I got rights. You can't treat me no different than you treated him." Jimmy's arrogance fairly leapt from his expression.

"This is about you, not Chuck. What's your understanding of what we expect about bein' on time, Jimmy?" Sonny asked.

> A performance problem exists when:
> - A pattern of misbehavior or poor results continues without sustained improvement.
> - Misbehavior is found to be intentional or malicious.
> - A behavior violates the law or shows disrespect for others or the company (fighting, theft, abusive language.

"You can expect what you want to. I wasn't as late as Chuck, so I'm just goin' on back to work now." He walked away. Sonny was flabbergasted.

Confront the 5% Behavior

"Jimmy!" Sonny called out as he walked to catch him, "You can't just walk off. I want you to come with me an' talk with Marty right now."

"The Constitution of the U.S. of A. says I got the right to free speech, and I don't want to talk to nobody, so I ain't goin',"* Jimmy said smugly.

"Well, the Constitution says citizens can keep and bear arms, but you ain't allowed to bring guns in *here*, are you?" Sonny replied. "This is a place of work, and the law allows us to regulate what you do in here. Right now, your assigned work is to come with me to Marty's office. If you don't, that's insubordination and you'll lose your job. It's your choice. You comin' with me, or not?"

"Well, I reckon if you put it like that," Jimmy said, mostly to the folks nearby who were watching.

A few minutes later, Marty listened to Sonny's explanation of Jimmy's behavior, which, under the circumstances, Marty thought was pretty calm. Looking at Jimmy, Marty said, "Jimmy, this is much more serious than tardiness. Why did you say that to Sonny?"

"Since you won't tell us how much we can be late, I'll just have to make my own rules," Jimmy said, "and I figure since Chuck was about 15 minutes late, you have to let us all be 15 minutes late."

"Jimmy, what do you understand our expectation on your attendance to be?"

"I told you: I ain't as bad as Chuck," Jimmy replied.

"That's not our expectation on attendance," Marty said. "We expect people to be here on time, every day..."

"But Chuck wasn't! That ain't fair!" Jimmy interrupted.

"Jimmy, let's get to the bottom line. Would it be fair to say that you don't fully agree with our expectation that people should be at work every day, on time?"

"That's right, 'cause it *ain't* fair."

"Understanding that you don't fully agree with it, are you willing to commit to meeting that expectation anyway?"

> Focus on behavior and commitment, not attitude, personality or the past.

Jimmy stiffened. This was a new and unexpected tactic. He could lie, or he could challenge. "You can expect what you want. I expect *you* to be fair," Jimmy said.

Marty frowned. "Jimmy, as I said, this is very serious. We've come to a point of decision for both of us. You have to decide whether you want to work here; because if you do, we need to see some lasting changes in your commitment starting immediately. Your behaviors in the areas of attendance and lack of respect for leaders are not acceptable. We both need some time to think this through carefully. I want you to take tonight to think it over and decide whether you want to make the commitment necessary to keep working here."

"I ain't resignin' if that's what you're gettin' at," Jimmy said.

"You don't have to, Jimmy," Marty said. "We hope you'll decide it's worth it to change because you're an experienced person. But if you don't, we have a decision to make, too.

"Here's what I suggest you do," Marty continued. "Here's a blank sheet of paper. Take some time and write on one side all the things you like about working here. Then, on the other side, write down all the things you *dis*like about working here. Look it over and see if it's worth it to change. If it is, we expect you to come up with a plan on how you will improve your performance and your commitment. We'll meet with you first thing tomorrow to go over your plan and make our decision."

"You gonna pay me overtime for doin' that?" Jimmy shot back.

Marty paused. He could see where this path was leading, but knew he had to provide due process. "The piece of paper is a suggestion, not a requirement. However, I expect you to be prepared to make a commitment and to explain how you plan to change your behavior. You have to make a choice."

"You'll go back to work now for the rest of the day," Marty said. "What actions do you think we expect of you for the rest of today and tonight?"

> Credible consequences work – emotions don't.

"You want me to be a good boy," Jimmy said, smirking.

Marty ignored the sarcasm. "In essence, that's right. I understand you aren't happy with this situation, but we expect you to finish the day with acceptable productivity and behavior if you want to stay employed. And," he added, "we intend to respect you by keeping this discussion private, and we expect that you'll do the same."

"Jimmy," Marty concluded, "I really hope you'll take this seriously, because I don't want you to lose your job, and that *will* be the result if you aren't prepared to commit to a plan for improvement we can accept. Then, we'll have to make a decision. See you in the morning."

After Jimmy's wordless exit, Marty turned to Sonny. "Well?" he asked.

"My nerves can't take many more like this," Sonny replied, wringing his hands. "I hope he quits."

30

Back on the floor, operators were talking about Sonny's encounter with Jimmy.

"Yeah, I think his rope's about run out," Sam had chimed in.

"Naw . . . he's beat worse than this before. He'll wriggle off the hook again," Henry pronounced with certainty. "What do you think, Chuck?"

Chuck just shrugged and walked away.

"Not quite his self today, is he?" Henry said.

No – that was obvious. His movements were slower, his eyes downcast, his shoulders a bit stooped. He acknowledged greetings but didn't pause to joke or chat.

Missy noticed the difference when Chuck came over to move her finished parts. He barely said hello, keeping his eyes on the task.

"Hey, Chuck, what're you so down in the mouth about?" Missy said.

"Oh, I'm OK," he replied unconvincingly.

"Come over here a minute." He obliged, and as they made eye contact, she said, "This ain't like you, mopin' around. What's up?"

"Just thinkin' about Jimmy's all," Chuck replied.

"Yeah. I saw him raggin' on you back there yesterday," Missy said empathetically. "But Chuck, you can't let him get you down."

"Well, that didn't bother me. I guess I feel bad that he got in trouble this mornin' 'cause a what I told him. Kinda hate to go back there and face him."

"Listen here, Chuck," she said, idling her machine

momentarily. "We've worked here a long time, and we both had our share of problems, ain't we?"

"Yeah, reckon we have," he said.

"Jimmy's responsible for his life. You can't control what he does. He's playin' a game that he might be about to lose, but you didn't cause his problems. Don't let what he does drag you down. Listen, buddy, I finally figured out that if this place is gonna make it, I'd better grab an oar and start rowin'. I think you're on board with me, 'cause I see you getting things picked up on time, keepin' after it all day, lookin' to help out the other operators, and cleaning the place up a little. Am I right, or is that your twin brother I been seeing?"

The corner of Chuck's mouth turned up a little in a half-smile as she looked into the center of his eyes. There was a clarity there she wasn't used to.

"Yep. You're right."

"Chuck, it's a trip to see what we can do when we put ourselves to it," Missy said. Then, turning away and muffling a laugh, she added, "Now, get it in gear and take that box out of here 'fore I get all mushy and puke."

31

"Ow!"

Marty's razor had claimed another patch of flesh as he readied for work the next morning. *"Tough night,"* he thought, recalling his fitful anticipation of the meeting with Jimmy in an hour. *'It had to be this way,'* he reflected on his action with Jimmy, *'but will the performance counseling method work?'* And, in his heart, he wondered what he really *wanted* to happen – improvement, or termination?

He wasn't sure he wanted to think too long on that one.

Later, outside the facility, he wordlessly threw his hand up in response to Bubba' greeting. Bubba knew what that meant. Marty was as nervous as a tabby cat at the hound dog trials. Sonny had been there for half an hour already, pacing a new path around the smoking area. *"This'll either kill Sonny or prove something to him,"* Bubba thought. Everybody knew, of course, the drama about to play out at Specialty Products; they had known within moments of the meeting yesterday. Like everyone else, Bubba went inside knowing that it would be over soon, one way or another.

Jimmy peeled into the parking lot at starting time on the nose. He had the clock tolerance down with mathematical precision. At one minute after starting time he hit the door. At two after he tossed his coat in the locker. At three after, on his way to the clock, a couple of his buddies stopped him. They looked a little concerned, but his gestures and laugh indicated 'No problem'. At five after he punched his card, then ambled for Marty's office, whistling leisurely. Nearby operators willed their machines to run more quietly as they waited for the show to begin.

Maintaining respect

Marty spotted him approaching and called, "Come in, Jimmy. We've been expecting you." In the room were Sonny and Marilyn, the HR Representative. *'This is big,'* Jimmy thought, noting disquietingly that they all seemed unusually calm.

"What's up, captain?" Jimmy said. He had a toothpick between his teeth, which he pulled out as he sat down.

"Well, that's our question for you. What thoughts did you have about your behavior yesterday, and about meeting our expectation on attendance and showing more respect to leadership?"

"You know, I was real busy last night with the company bowling league. We're in first place, you know. But I decided I want to keep my job," Jimmy grinned, "so all you have to do is tell me how much I can be out, and I'm yours."

"Jimmy, who is responsible for your being at work on time?" Marty asked.

"I reckon I am," Jimmy replied cautiously.

"So, who's the only person who can improve your performance?" Sonny said.

"I don't know if anybody can, since y'all won't tell me how much I can miss," said Jimmy, "and since you're so inconsistent. Chuck can be late and nothing's said to him..."

"That ain't true," Sonny said. "We did talk to Chuck, and he told us how he was gonna fix his problem. You ain't committed to do nothin'."

Marty resumed control with a look toward Sonny, then proceeded. "Jimmy, are you prepared to tell us your plan to improve your attendance and meet the expectation?"

"Look, what you see is what you get. It's your job to plan."

"And what's *your* job, Jimmy?"

"To do what you tell me," Jimmy said.

"And we asked you to come prepared with a plan this morning. Is that what you heard?"

"Yeah, but like I said..."

"So, you're telling me that you're *not* prepared with a plan to meet the expectation?"

I reckon not. It ain't fair."

"Then, it's obvious to me that you are unlikely to meet the expectation. Would you agree?"

> Key question: What is the likelihood of lasting improvement?

"You do what you gotta do, and I'll do what I gotta do." Jimmy looked down at the floor, sneaked a peek at Marty under his hat brim, and returned to his downward stare.

"Jimmy, based on your behavior of yesterday toward Sonny, your repeated disrespectful behavior today and your lack of commitment to meet our expectation on attendance, your employment here will end as of today."

"You can't do that..." Jimmy started.

"Jimmy, it's over," Marty said firmly. "The only remaining question is how you want it reflected on your record. Since your reason for dismissal didn't involve gross misconduct or violence, we will offer you a chance to resign if you want."

"What good's that?" Jimmy said, "and what about my unemployment?"

"I don't think it's necessary to kick you on your way out," Marty said. "Although your behavior isn't acceptable, you're a person just like me. If it were me, I'd rather tell people I quit, and not have to lie about it."

> Maintain respect at termination, even for those not deserving it.

> Fairness is based on consistency of the process, not simply outcomes.

Marilyn finally spoke up. "As far as unemployment, we don't make that determination; the state does. You'll apply for benefits at the state office, and they'll ask your reason for leaving. You tell them it's a requested resignation, and they'll verify it with us. Then, they'll decide if your case fits their standards."

"I'm sorry it came to this, Jimmy," said Marty. "Believe it or not, I really am."

Ensure Accountability

- A performance problem exists when:
  - A pattern of misbehavior or continuing poor results without sustained improvement.
  - Misbehavior is found to be intentional and/or malicious.
  - A behavior violates laws or shows disrespect for others or the company (fighting, stealing, abusive language, etc.).
- To deal with problem behaviors:
  - Ensure awareness of the problem and understanding of the impact
  - Give them a chance to explain; listen actively and ask open-ended questions.
  - Ask for their commitment to a specific change.
  - Help them develop a specific action plan that brings good intentions to life.
  - Support good faith tries, even if they stumble.
  - Focus on behavior nor attitude, personality, or the past.
- Achieving Results
  - Ask yourself the key question: Based on their behavior and commitment, what is the likelihood of lasting improvement?
  - Stay Calm: Credible consequences work – emotion doesn't.
  - Maintain Respect even at termination, even for those not acting respectfully.
  - Fairness is based on consistency of process, (similar consequences for similar behavior) not simply the outcome.

GETTING RESULTS

It takes time and effort to create change but staying the same guarantees failure.

****

If you want to run with the big dogs, you gotta get off the porch – Bubba

---

32

It had been four months since Jimmy's departure; not quite six since implementing the new approach. Time for the dog and pony show: Frank the VP was here to check results. Tom came along; the first time he'd graced Smyrna with his presence. He started the day with complaints about his room at the Smyrna House Inn. Frank ignored him.

Barb's tour went well. Frank quickly put her at ease, and she pointed out the method improvements employees had developed. Next, the managers met in the training room to review progress.

"Here's the reason we're ahead of budget," Marty said. "More than 96 percent at work each day, on time – and those are accurate numbers. More than 47 percent have perfect attendance for six months. That's a miracle compared to what it was last year."

"How many did you fire to get this, Marty?" Tom chimed in sarcastically. He knew the answer but seemed to revel in the power to ask the question.

"As you know, Tom, there are three employees who

are no longer working here. Two resigned voluntarily because they could see that they would not be able to meet our expectation, and one resignation was requested. And, as I discussed with Frank, the assembly supervisor resigned last week because he wouldn't manage with our approach."

"And sir, if you don't mind my buttin' in," Sonny said, "the ones that left don't explain the turnaround. It's the ones who *stayed* and improved their performance that's made the difference."

"It makes it easier on those who were *always* here every day, too," Marty added. "They can be more productive since they don't have to pick up slack for those who are out."

Frank nodded. "Guys, you've made quite an improvement. What's next?"

"Our goal is to sustain attendance at between 98 and 99 percent, year in and year out. In fact, that isn't a goal; it's an expectation."

"So, based on your 95-5 philosophy, you just got rid of the 5 percent that were dragging you down, right?" said Tom.

"No, that's not it at all," Marty said. "We don't focus on the 5 percent's behaviors; we deal with them. Our focus is on the 95 percent."

"Some say everybody's got a little 5 percenter in 'em," Sonny said, "or in my case, a little more than 5." Everybody chuckled, even Tom.

Marty added, "It's not the people who are the problem. It's the way we lead people; the systems and procedures which let the 5 percent control what we can achieve. Our focus is to improve the system for us all. We just want to involve the people who know the job best."

After the session, Marty asked Frank and Tom to come to his office. "You know that Vince quit as assembly supervisor," he said. "I'd like to promote Bubba Self to that position."

"Well," Frank said, "that's an interesting choice. He's the set-up technician, right?"

"Any assembly experience?" asked Tom.

"No. But guys, he has one characteristic that we desperately need: leadership," Marty said. "He's perceptive, he communicates well even under pressure, and he has high expectations. He's a big reason we've come this far. He learned the machine set-up role very quickly, and I expect he can learn assembly just as quickly."

"Well, Marty, it's your plant," Frank said. "You've done well so far. Why should I grab the reins from you now?"

33

The next few weeks were busy for Bubba as he learned his new job. As he learned the technical processes of Assembly, Bubba also learned the strengths of each of his employees. His openness, humor and willingness to listen earned him respect – even though his occasional mistakes gave his employees something to rib him about.

He'd seen Marty in the brief production meetings each Monday morning. He was surprised when Marty Appeared, daybook in hand, in the Assembly department one morning.

"Checkin' in on me?" Bubba called.

"Yeah . . . I mean, no . . . not the way your mean," Marty stammered. "I've been thinking. Frank's right. The real challenge will be to maintain our improvements over a long period. It's easy to forget how bad we were, and to take for granted how far we've come."

"Guess you're right." Bubba said. "Whatcha got in the book this time?"

"First, I've tried to summarize what we expect of people," Marty said. "See what you think of this Code of Conduct.

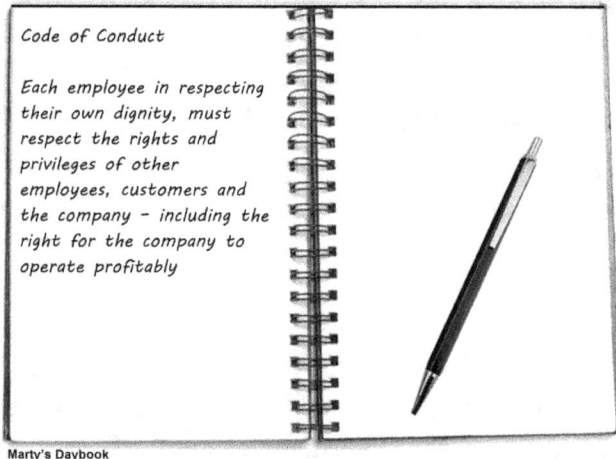

Marty's Daybook

Code of Conduct

Each employee in respecting their own dignity, must respect the rights and privileges of other employees, customers and the company – including the right for the company to operate profitably

"I like that," Bubba replied. "It sorta gives folks one rule to live by."

"That's the idea. I also think I've developed sort of a monitoring system to help keep us on track," Marty said.

Kinda like dashboard on a car – to tell you what's happenin' under the hood?" asked bubba.

"Yeah. That's a good illustration," Marty said. "Take a look at these gauges.

The pages read:

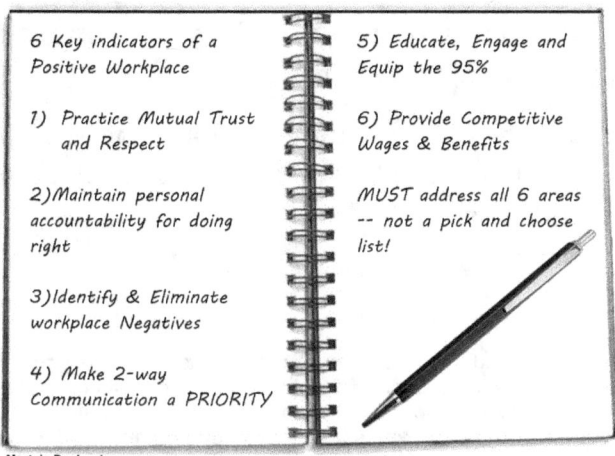

6 Key indicators of a Positive Workplace

1) Practice Mutual Trust and Respect

2) Maintain personal accountability for doing right

3) Identify & Eliminate workplace Negatives

4) Make 2-way Communication a PRIORITY

5) Educate, Engage and Equip the 95%

6) Provide Competitive Wages & Benefits

MUST address all 6 areas -- not a pick and choose list!

Marty's Daybook

"You mean, if we keep on doing these things, we'll have a good place to work?" Bubba asked

"Yes, I think so," said Marty. "They all tie together. Think about it: Can you hold people accountable for doing right without showing them trust and respect every day? Will people want to learn and be involved if our wages aren't competitive?"

"And listen' to folks is really the key, I think," said Bubba. "It shows 'em you care about them as people, not just workers."

"Leaders have to also constantly look for negatives that hold people back from performing their best, too," Marty concluded.

And the people doin' the job know the job best, like you always told me, so it pays to listen to 'em," Bubba agreed. "I think you pretty well got it figured out."

"Partly thanks to you Bubba," Marty said.

"Folks like me may not be too smoot, but we've seen a thing or two over the years," Bubba said. "I'm real glad we finally got someone to listen."

"I'm just glad I finally got smart enough to listen." Marty responded. "You know, when you think about it, it's just common sense."

Getting Things Done
by Tom Peters
Author of: *In Search of Excellence*

Most grand strategies flop. Most change programs fizzle. Why? We worry too much about the plan – and not enough about implementation. Looking back on 35 years or so of being managed, managing, and observing organizations, I offer a few top implementers' secrets:

Listening. You'll invariably find answers – if your ears are open. The average boss is a better talker than listener. On the other hand, peak performers in any role may be close to inarticulate – but absorb a million details of what's on other folks' minds. They act accordingly.

Curiosity. Never stop asking: "Can you help me understand this better?" "Can you give me an example?" Can you direct me to the person closest to the action?"

Information. Forget information overload. All people crave information and being "in the loop." The informed person is empowered person. The uninformed person is unempowered.

"Talk the walk". You've heard of "walk the talk." but organization researcher Karl Weick insists the revers is even mor important. The leader's chief role is to add coherence to the ambiguous real world. That happens only when the boss hangs out, observes – and then explains, vividly, what they've seen and what it means in the larger scheme of things.

Just Do It. The reason most plans are a joke is that, in truth, nobody knows nothin' about nothin'. So, the only way we can make progress is to do something – and then see what happens.

Life is not about serenely walking down the middle of spick-and-span streets. It's about veering to and fro, bouncing off guardrails, then overcorrecting. But you can't correct a course until you've taken to the road!

34

This Friday night was a festive time for the Self family. They were celebrating Bubba's promotion and their son Tom had won the annual award for citizenship at Smyrna High School. With his gift certificate for two large pizzas, he treated the family for a night out.

"Son, I'm proud of you," Bubba said. "I know it ain't easy doing right when everybody else ain't."

"Yes, sir. Coach Hill said he had a lot of respect for the way I handled that smokin' thing. Said it took guts to admit I was there when the others wouldn't. I think he's about as proud for me to get this award as you are."

"Yeah, 'cause he sure can't be proud of your jump shot," teased his sister, Megan.

As they laughed, they heard a call from across the restaurant. "Hey, boss-man, what y'all doin' here with the workin' folks?" It was Junior. Missy was with him.

"Come on and sit down, rascal," said Bubba, "but don't touch this pizza my boy got for us."

As Missy and Dot chatted, Junior leaned over to Bubba. "I finished my rehab – at least the first part. Ain't had a drop of nothing for nearly six months."

"You're still goin' to support group, right?"

"Yep. That's a lifetime commitment," Junior replied.

"Speakin' of commitment, what about you and . . ." Bubba nodded in Missy's direction.

"Naw. Not yet, leastways. It took us a long time to get back together, and we want to be sure this time. But at least her momma's speakin' to me now that I'm sober."

"That's always a good sign," Bubba chuckled. "Now, when mama wants to move in with you . . ."

"Whoa, boy! Ain't nobody movin' nowhere 'less we get married. I got *myself* clean, but my *house* is another thing," Junior joked. "Hey, guess who I saw today? Ol' Jimmy Sullivan."

"Yeah? What's that sorry cuss doin'?"

"Lookin' for a job, mostly, since y'all wised up to him. He's done tried everywhere in town. Even *we* won't hire him. He's got to where he can't afford a beer at the Palace."

"You ain't *going* to the Palace, are you?" Bubba asked, suddenly serious.

"No. I can't hang out there no more. That's part of how I plan to stay sober. But I call Roy pretty regular to catch up on all the news in town."

"Good." Bubba looked at his brother. "I'm proud of you, Junior."

"Yep. I'm pretty pleased myself," he grinned, grabbing an iced tea glass from a passing waitress. "Here's to us, bro. Two workin' men trying to keep it in the road."

"And holdin' our own or a little better, I'd say," Bubba nodded.

FINAL THOUGHTS

While some would say that Bubba's wisdom is simple – even simplistic – it is surprisingly difficult to reduce the process of creating a positive workplace to a few "steps." The techniques illustrated in this book are based on a philosophy: that the workplace system must be designed around the interests and concerns of the dependable and conscientious majority of employees, not the malicious 5%.

Philosophies aren't always neat, orderly, or easy to articulate. Obviously, without a deep commitment to your conscientious employees, nothing in the book makes sense. But beliefs must drive actions, or they become merely good intentions. For change to be effective, it must address both formal policies and individual behavior.

It is easy to understate the importance of a system, yet it can facilitate or hinder supervisors in "doing the right thing." Often, organizations train their supervisors and are disappointed with the results – the trained supervisors don't do anything differently. Supervisors would like to apply what they've learned, but existing policies can make it difficult. Similarly, merely changing policies without changing problem behaviors will not change workplace results. It isn't enough to train people; you must also make sure the system supports their efforts.

In short, individual behaviors and workplace systems must complement the 95/5 philosophy in order for the workplace to operate effectively.

Although Bubba's story is underpinned with real incidents, it is fictional; thus, we have included three actual case studies in Appendix B to illustrate how businesses at different locations and times applied these principles successfully.

STEPS TO A POSITIVE WORKPLACE	Or as Bubba says . . .
Recognize the impact of the system - On the decent majority and - On the 5% who are game players	Most people want to do what's right. But they get fed up.
Pursue change – understand that change is a process, not an event.	Folks ain't opposed to change – when they can ss what's in it for them.
Redesign the system based on high expectations. - Identify and eliminate negatives in the system. - Demonstrate mutual trust and respect in your actions. - Create opportunities for involvement and overcome obstacles through active listening.	Lots of folks want to make things better. They're just waitin' for the bosses to listen.
Ensure accountability for doing right – for yourself and others.	If people give better, they oughta get better.
Measure results. Set tangible targets for improvement: - Attendance - Productivity/throughput - Waste/Errors - Safety, etc.	If you always do what you've always done, you'll always get what you've always gotten.
Watch six key indicators to keep your culture on track: - Actions that show mutual trust and respect - Personal accountability - Identify and eliminate negatives - Two-way communication - Engage, equip and enable employees - Competitive wages and benefits	You gotta keep paying attention 'cause it ain't ever finished.

BUBBA ON BUSINESS

APPENDIX A

But What About . . . ?

Do these concepts work in the real world?

Yes. The concepts have been around at least since Moses, but we aren't that old. For the past 40 years, we have seen them work in new facilities and existing ones; in previously 'OK" environments as well as in poor ones. See Appendix B for details on measurable outcomes. In addition to the dollars-and-cents improvement, you'll notice subtle differences in workplace behaviors – people helping others without being asked and offering ideas and committing to work on them.

What are the keys to success?

First, leaders have to approach the concepts as values to be lived out, not as a "program" to fix something broken. You have to genuinely believe that the vast majority of people want to do a good job, and make your decisions based on that belief. That's not as easy as it sounds. You can't fake it; people can smell a phony. Second, it helps to have a reasonably healthy market forecast for your product or services for the coming months. It sounds a bit hollow to talk about mutual trust and respect and commitment and accountability when you are routinely laying off employees.

Finally, if your work relationships are in deep trouble now, you will need to build bridges first – don't try to make these changes in the midst of labor negotiations or a strike, for example. No one will believe you're sincere.

How long does it take?

We can't generalize. It depends on how good or bad the environment is, how committed the leadership team is, how much investment can be dedicated to it, how flexible the work process is to allow for employee involvement, and so on. As the story indicated, you can see results from little improvements almost immediately upon implementation. Bigger changes (like attendance) take more time to plan and get approvals, but once implemented, get results almost immediately. Most should see a sustainable, big difference in six months to a year.

I like some of the ideas in the book, but others I question. Is it an all or nothing deal?

No. We've never had two clients take the exact same course and implement every concept or policy in the exact same way. You have to look at what you feel are your biggest "hurts". The real goal is for each organization to examine their own practices in light of the Six Key Indicators in outline in Chapter 32 in Marty's Daybook notes. Then you can decide your priorities and decide what changes to make and in what order. One hint; the more people you can involve, the more buy-in and trust you build – the less time it will take.

Specialty Products didn't have a union. Will these concepts work in an organization with a union?

Yes, People are people; despite stereotypes, most union members are 95%-ers. We've seen success in unionized facilities, but involvement of the local union leadership is key, even if the changes won't affect terms that are negotiated. Leaders are still responsible for determining how they will treat people – as badly as they are legally permitted, or with the respect they want for themselves. We found that, when you ask managers and union leaders separately what kind of workplace they want, the answers are the same.

This stuff sounds too soft. You don't know the kind of people we have – they on give the minimum.

You're right, we don't know the people you work with, but we'd still bet the vast majority of workers at all levels are decent human beings that will respond positively when treated with trust and respect. Some of them may have given up a little of their self-respect because the workplace systems made that a rational choice. Unfortunately, in many organizations high performance is not rational, all it gets you is more and harder work, while low performers are tolerated and "get by with murder." Ant it's true that society has changed in recent year. Personal accountability isn't automatically instilled at home or school anymore, so we have to establish it at work. Again though, our experience suggests that the vast majority of people entering the workforce are basically decent and will respond with their best efforts for a company that treats them with respect. People tend to live up to or down to expectations. So, if you have an organization that expects the best from their employees you will more likely get their best. It is leadership's job to help the 5% that choose not to make or keep commitments find a way to change or find a way out.

One last point, don't misunderstand 'respect' to mean 'permissiveness.' Sometimes the most respectful thing you can do is tell a person his or her behavior is out of bounds and can't continue. In a positive workplace, you set high standard and hold people to be accountable. A positive workplace isn't necessarily and easy place to work, just a good one.

I like the ideas, but corporate won't let me. . . the union won't let me. . . my boss won't let me. . .

We get the picture. What was it that Bubba said – "it's easy to find reasons not to do something"? All authority is delegated from somewhere, and no manager is free to do whatever he or she wants. However, you can control how you will personally treat people. Start by removing some annoyances you can control that keep people from doing a good job.

> A journey of 1000 miles begins with a single step –
> *Chinese Proverb*

APPENDIX B
Measuring Results

How can you objectively measure progress in creating an effective workplace? Obviously, gains in "morale" are subjective and intangible, but they're clearly visible – especially when you have problems.

One area which most companies *can* measure is **attendance**; however, it isn't as easy as you think to compare "apples to apples". You see, many companies don't "count" every absence – it's tough to think about how bad things really *are*.

For example: some "point systems" give only *one* point for consecutive days missed. This is intended to keep from penalizing people who are legitimately sick, with the idea that "real" illnesses will last more than one day. However, they end up penalizing people who try to come back from an illness too early and relapse. Other companies institute "mini-leaves" for the same reason: each day counts as a point, *unless* you miss five days in a row; then, it counts "zero". Rationally, if you had to be out a couple of days, would you come back to work the next day under that system? And some "no fault" systems really aren't no fault, because they require a doctor's note to excuse an absence.

All these "modifications" came about when a "hard nosed" system negatively impacted a good performer, and the organization believed an exception was needed. You see the problem for measurement: it's hard to get a true "baseline" when you switch from a system which *doesn't* count some absences to one which that records *every* absence on a *scheduled* work day (exceptions may be breavement, jury/civic duty, and vacation because attendance is not scheduled; absences on overtime *are* counted, because it's scheduled work time) and looks for *patterns* of abuse instead of *incidents* or *occurrences*.

Even with these difficulties, it's still possible to measure attendance improvement in most organizations.

Another "objective" measurement of progress is **turnover** – people are more likely to stay at a workplace which treats them as responsible adults. Turnover is a bit more complex than attendance, because there are many good reasons someone might leave a company – moving from the area; change in family circumstances (divorce, marriage, spouse's promotion, birth of a child); need for a different work schedule; military service or educational opportunity; an industry that's up-and-down; even a 'mid-life crisis'. "More money" is often cited as a 'good' reason for leaving, but our experience is that in many cases, that's just a socially acceptable excuse. The real question for a company is, "Why were they *looking*?" While money is important to everyone, we see countless cases where people leave higher-paying jobs to come to work in a positive environment. As one such interviewee said, "We've finally figured it out – they're paying us more than the job is worth so they can treat us like crap."* (On the other hand, you can't pay the lowest possible wages and have a positive environment – look at the last 'Key Indicators' in the chart at the end of Chapter 33).

Certainly, "treating people the way you want to be treated" is more than an economic issue. However, business legitimately uses dollars to measure value – and clearly, by that measure, there are tangible rewards for improving the workplace environment.

APPENDIX C

Ways to Get Started

Obviously, each business is different. Where you start depends on your history of trust or distrust; your company's 'personality'; the problems you face; the resources you have. Here's a list of ideas – some risky, some tame; some difficult, some easy – that others have used to start the change process by **creating awareness** and **developing understanding**.

Have your leadership team read this book, then discuss it. Evaluate your organization against the Six Key Indicators. Ask your fellow employees some key questions like:

– What percentage of people do you really believe is basically decent?

– Who do you think our company policies are most designed for: the 95% or the 5%?

– Do you feel like the company really treats most people like responsible adults? Do most of our people deserve to be treated like adults?

– Are there some people who always try to take advantage of situations? Is it mostly the same people? How committed do you think they are to their job? What should we do with those people?

– Should everybody be treated equally, regardless of their past behavior?

Start a series of "skip-level" meetings with employees. Listen to the negatives that concern them. One caveat: if you haven't done this before, you may hear the verbal equivalent of 'throwing up' at first – trivial issues, impossible demands, or hostility designed to test your commitment. Don't make commitments for change too hastily, but listen and ask them why these are important. This will pass, and people will move to more basic issues

Identify one major issue involving people which, if solved, would dramatically impact your bottom line. Brainstorm non-conventional ways to tackle this based on Bubba's principles.

Conduct an employee opinion survey – but only if you're willing to report results honestly and act on the things you discover.

Walk around the facility. Find some "95 percenters" and ask them about "the one thing they would do if they were plant manager".

Eat lunch at a large table in the break room/cafeteria once a week. Specifically invite new faces each time. Talk about orders, customers, new products/equipment, or just what people have done today at work. Listen to the questions they ask and topics they bring up.

Have an off-site meeting for your managers and, if unionized, the union committee. Discuss what kind of workplace you really want, and what obstacles are in your way.

Assemble a policy review team to look at one of your major policies (like attendance or discipline) or your entire handbook. Ask, "How would I feel if this were applied to *me*?" Look for policies designed around the 5%, and refocus them on the 95%.

If you decide to change a major policy, talk individually with everyone you can. Discuss how the change would affect them. Discuss concerns honestly; ask them for support.

> "The best time to plant a tree was 20 years ago. The second-best time is today."
> - Chinese proverb

Identify one or more "bottom performers". Analyze what behaviors they display; how those differ from expectations; and what consequences they have gotten for them. Develop a plan to meet with them and discuss changes they are willing to make.

WHO WROTE THIS BOOK?

David Dunn is the source of many of the book's examples and situations. He draws on his experience with dozens of clients as a consultant, first with The Thompson Group and then with Ninety-Five/Five, plus his years as a first-line supervisor and a Human Resources professional in a manufacturing environment.

Dennis Melton developed the book's story, characters and dialog. Prior to becoming a principal in Ninety-Five/Five, he worked in organization development and employee/leadership communications for a major telecom equipment manufacturer; and in video, advertising and marketing for a satellite system manufacturer and a non-profit organization.

How do I contact the authors?

Email: ddunn@95-5consultingservices.com **or** call us at (615) 289-9505

www.ingramcontent.com/pod-product-compliance
Lightning Source LLC
Chambersburg PA
CBHW071411210526
45465CB00001B/339